Excel 2010
Foundation to Expert Guide

Chris Voyse and Patrice Muse

Published by
Voyse Recognition Limited

177634 ✓

NL 005.54 EXC

Excel
Spreadsheets
Excel 2010
Computers

© 2010 Voyse Recognition Limited

This guide has been designed in order to create a methodical approach to learning this product. www.smart-pc-guides.com outlines all the guides in the Office 2010 portfolio.

Notice of Liability

First Published in Great Britain in 2010

Voyse Recognition Limited
Smart PC Guides
Century Business Centre
Manvers Way
Manvers
Rotherham
South Yorkshire
S63 5DA
01709 300188

ISBN 978 1 905657 469

Section 1: Foundation Level Objectives

Section 2: Intermediate Level Objectives

Section 3: Expert Level Objectives

Section 1

Foundation Level Objectives

Note: If you are working in Windows XP instead of Windows Vista or Windows 7, dialog boxes may look different but function in a similar way.

Table of Contents

Introducing the Excel Screen

Excel 2010 is a simple and efficient spreadsheet application released by Microsoft that runs in a Windows environment allowing the user to create and edit both small and large workbooks. It is user-friendly and easy to work with providing prompts to help the user identify icons on the screen that the user maybe unfamiliar with and takes the user through the various functions within this application.

Tour of the Screen

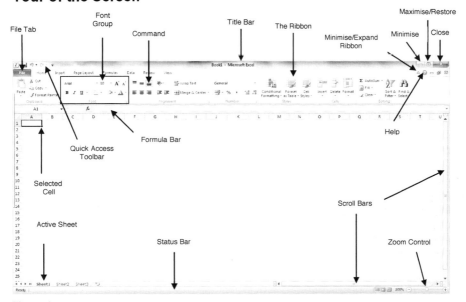

Figure 1

File Tab

In Excel 2010 the File Tab ![File] replaces the Office button and the File menu used in earlier versions of Excel. Clicking on the File Tab takes you to the Backstage view where files and data about them are managed, for example creating, saving, and setting options. The File Tab also displays the commands for Save, Save As, Open, Close, Info, Recent, New, Print, Save & Send, Help, Options and Exit.

Title Bar

The Title Bar is highlighted at the top of the screen and defines the programme that the user is in and the name of the Excel Workbook that the user has open. Excel will automatically display the default name, for example Book 1, in the Title Bar. Once the workbook has been saved, the saved name will be displayed in the Title Bar.

The Ribbon

The Ribbon is the control centre that quickly helps the user locate the commands needed to complete a task and is organised into three parts:

Core Tasks

Consisting of seven tabs: Home, Insert, Page Layout, Formulas, Data, Review and View

Groups

Related items grouped together

Commands

Buttons, boxes and menus that give instruction

The Ribbon organises the commands into logical groups all collected together under the Tabs with each Tab relating to a type of activity.

To minimise the Ribbon double click with the left button on the active Tab, for example Home , the Ribbon and its commands disappear. To display the Ribbon and its commands, click with the left button on any one of the Tabs. Alternatively, CTRL F1 minimises/maximises the ribbon.

Help

The Help icon can be found on the right hand side of the Ribbon.

Formula Bar

The Formula Bar is used for creating formula and displays the active cell.

Scroll Bars

Horizontal and Vertical scroll bars enable users to move around the workbook.

Sheet Tab

The Sheet Tab ‖ ◄ ► ‖ Sheet1 Sheet2 Sheet3 displays in white the active worksheet.

Page Layout View

Page Layout view makes it easy to add headers and footers as well as adjust and turn margins on and off. Page Layout view enables the user to view the workbook as it will appear on a printed page. To activate Page Layout view:

1. Click the View Tab, select Page Layout Page Layout

2. Alternatively using the keyboard shortcuts press ALT W P

3. Or select the Page Layout view icon in the Status Bar

Status Bar

The Status Bar is found at the bottom of the worksheet window and can be customised to display the features that the user wants to see. To customise the Status Bar

1. Press the right  button on the Status Bar, the Customise Status Bar menu appears

Customize Status Bar	
✓ Cell Mode	Ready
✓ Signatures	Off
✓ Information Management Policy	Off
✓ Permissions	Off
Caps Lock	Off
Num Lock	On
✓ Scroll Lock	Off
✓ Fixed Decimal	Off
Overtype Mode	
✓ End Mode	
Macro Recording	Not Recording

Figure 2

2. To activate the Caps Lock so it is displayed in the Status Bar when in use

3. Click with the left button on Caps Lock

4. A tick ✓ is displayed to indicate the feature has been activated

5. Click back in the worksheet

6. Press the CAPS key on the keyboard

7. Caps Lock is displayed in the Status Bar to show that it is activated

8. Click the CAPS key on the keyboard a second time to switch the feature off

Quick Access Toolbar

The Quick Access Toolbar can be found in the top section of the screen. It allows the user to display commands that are regularly used and that are independent of their associated Tabs.

Zoom Control

To use the Zoom Control drag with the left button to increase (magnify) or decrease the worksheet to display the information larger or smaller on screen.

Opening Microsoft Excel

To open the Excel 2010 application, select the Start Button , move the mouse pointer and pause over ▶ All Programs , click with the left button on Microsoft Office , move the mouse pointer and pause over Microsoft Excel 2010 , click with the right button, select Send to ▶, choose Desktop (create shortcut) . A shortcut key appears on the desktop Microsoft Excel 2010. Click with the left button on Microsoft Excel 2010 to open the programme.

Creating a shortcut to the desktop enables quick access to an application, folder or file; the shortcut can be identified by the arrow on the icon.

Understanding Worksheets

Each new workbook contains three worksheets, if more worksheets are required

1. Click on the File Tab, select Options

2. The Excel Options dialog appears

Figure 3

3. Alternatively press ALT   F   T

4. Choose the option - When creating new workbooks

5. Select - Include this many **s**heets

6. Type in the number of sheets required or use the arrow keys

Include this many sheets: 5

7. Press [OK] to set the new default number of worksheets

8. Select the [File] Tab, click [New]

9. Choose [Create] ,the new default worksheets appear

10. Alternatively, double click with the left button on [Blank workbook]

Moving Around Within a Worksheet

Excel references by a column reference and then a row reference. There are 16,384 columns and 1,048,576 rows in a worksheet.

1. Click in cell A1

2. Both the column and row references are highlighted in orange

Figure 4

3. The Formula Bar above column A displays the cell **A1**

4. When you select a cell a white cross ⊕ appears

5. To select a cell, click with the left button

6. There are a number of ways to move to a different cell

7. Use the arrow keys on the keyboard [↓] [↑] [→] [←]

8. This will highlight the next cell reference

9. The cell reference is displayed in the Formula Bar

10. Alternatively press the [TAB] key, the new active cell is displayed

11. To move back a cell, hold down [SHIFT] press the [TAB] key

12. Click on cell A1 using the left button

13. Hold down [CTRL], press [→] to display the final column in the worksheet

14. To return to column A1, hold down ◻ CTRL ◻ , press ◻ ⟵ ◻
15. In cell A1 hold the ◻ CTRL ◻ key down and select ◻ ↓ ◻
16. To return to cell A1 hold the ◻ CTRL ◻ key down and select ◻ ↑ ◻

Inserting Information into a Cell

1. When the mouse pointer ⬚ is moved in a cell a white cross appears ✛
2. Move the mouse pointer ⬚ over cell G2
3. Click with the left ⬚ button to select cell G2
4. Type out the word January
5. As text is typed the information appears in the Formula Bar and the cell

| G2 | ▾ | f_x | January |

Figure 5

6. To accept the information in G2 click on the blue tick ✓
7. Alternatively, press the ◻ Enter ◻ key on the keyboard
8. Text entered into a cell automatically aligns to the left ◻January◻

Editing Information

Excel 2010 allows the user to change information in several different ways.

To go back a character, use the ◻ BACK SPACE ◻ key on the keyboard.

1. Select the cell to be edited
2. Press ◻ F2 ◻ a flashing cursor appears, edit the cell contents as necessary
3. Alternatively move the mouse over the cell you want to edit
4. As you move over the cell a white cross appears ✛
5. Guide the white cross over the cell to be edited
6. Double click with the left ⬚ button
7. A flashing cursor appears where the cross was guided to appear
8. Edit the cell contents as necessary

Editing Information using the Formula Bar

1. Select the cell you want to edit

2. Move the left 🖱 button into the Formula Bar

3. Click with the left 🖱 button where the flashing cursor is to appear

E3	▾	f_x	Smart PC Guides

Figure 6

4. Once edited click on the blue tick ✓ or press the ⬛Enter⬛ key

Exercise 1: - Creating and Saving a Workbook

	A	B	C
1	Monthly Household Expenses		
2	Mortgage		£259.00
3	Rates		£27.00
4	Gas		£7.99
5	Electricity		£13.00
6	Phone		£15.00
7	Insurance		£8.50
8	Television		£16.99
9	Food		£120.00
10			
11	Total		£467.48

1. Open a new workbook by clicking on the **File** Tab

2. Select **New**, choose **Blank workbook**, click **Create**

3. Recreate the text shown in Exercise 1 above

4. Select the cell containing the title Monthly Household Expenses

5. Press the Bold icon **B** , click the left 🖱 button on the **File** Tab

6. Select the Save As icon **Save As** , the Save As dialog box appears

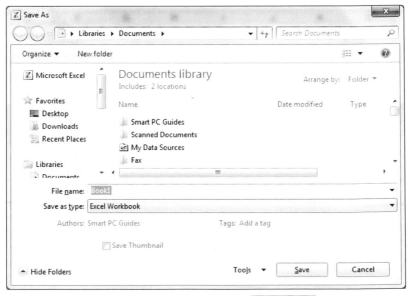

7. Type Expenses in the File **n**ame box, select **Save**

8. The Title Bar at the top of the screen now displays the named workbook

Saving a Workbook

There are occasions when a workbook needs to be saved in a different format, for example if a file needs to be saved in an earlier version format, Excel 97-2003.

1. Click on the **File** Tab, choose [🗷 Save As]

2. Alternatively press [F12] on the keyboard

3. The Save As dialog box appears

4. In the File name area type Expenses

5. In the Save as type box click on the downward pointing arrow

6. Select Excel 97-2003 Workbook, click [Save]

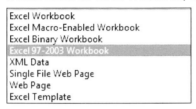

```
Excel Workbook
Excel Macro-Enabled Workbook
Excel Binary Workbook
Excel 97-2003 Workbook
XML Data
Single File Web Page
Web Page
Excel Template
```

Figure 7

Save a Workbook as a PDF

A workbook can be saved as a PDF (Portable Document Format); that is a fixed layout format and is a useful method of saving a workbook that is intended to be read and printed but not modified. To read a PDF the user will need to have Acrobat Reader installed on the computer.

1. Select **File**, [🗷 Save As]

2. In the File name box type Expenses

3. The Save as type area defaults as an Excel Workbook

4. Using the arrow key scroll down and select PDF

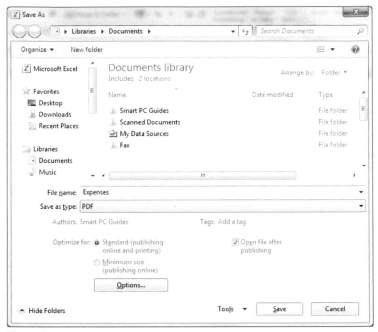

Figure 8

5. Choose Optimise for: select Standard (publishing online and printing)

6. Click with the left 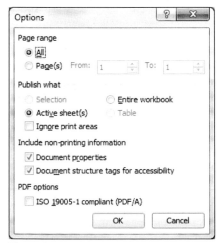 button on | Options... |

Figure 9

7. The Options dialog box appears, click | OK |, | Save |

8. The PDF is displayed that can be read and printed but not modified

Saving Workbooks in Different Formats

There may be occasions when a workbook needs to be saved in a different format, for example if a file needs to be saved in an earlier version format, Excel 97-2003.

1. Click **File**, choose ⬚ Save As

2. Alternatively press F12 on the keyboard

3. The Save As dialog box appears

4. In the File name area type Expenses

5. In the Save as type box click on the downward pointing arrow

6. Select Excel 97-2003 Workbook, click Save

> Excel Workbook
> Excel Macro-Enabled Workbook
> Excel Binary Workbook
> Excel 97-2003 Workbook
> XML Data
> Single File Web Page
> Web Page
> Excel Template

Figure 10

Opening a Workbook

1. Click on **File**, select 📂 Open

2. The Documents Library displays the files in My Documents area

3. Click with the left 🖱 button on the required workbook

4. Press the Enter key to open the workbook

5. Alternatively hold down the CTRL key, press the letter O to take the user to the Documents Library

Adjust the Number of Recently used Files

1. Select the **File** Tab

2. Choose 📄 Options , Advanced

3. The Excel Options dialog box appears

4. Scroll down and choose the option named Display

Display

Show this number of Recent Documents: 25

Figure 11

5. The default setting is 25, this can be increased to display 50

6. In the Show this number of <u>R</u>ecent Documents area

7. Type the number of documents to be displayed, click [OK]

8. To confirm that the new default is activated

9. Select the [File] Tab, choose [Recent]

10. The new default is displayed at the bottom of the screen

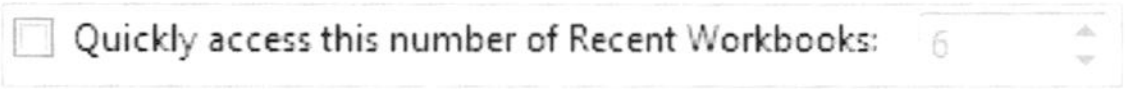

☐ Quickly access this number of Recent Workbooks: 6   ▲▼

Figure 12

11. Click with the left  button in the Quick Access area

12. A tick ☑ appears

13. The workbooks are displayed below the [File] Tab

🔲 Working with Diffe...

🔲 Expenses

Figure 13

Opening Workbooks using the Mouse

1. Select **File** , click 🖿 Open , the Open dialog box appears

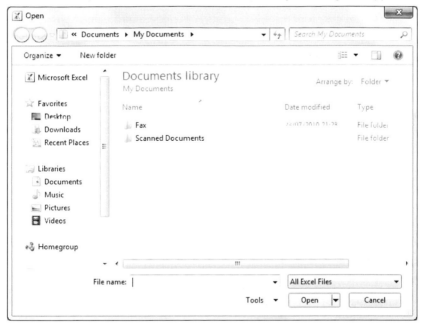

Figure 14

2. Choose ▷ ▪ Documents or the drive that contains the workbook

3. Double click with the left 🖱 button to open the required folder

4. Or click the left 🖱 button on the individual workbook, press Open ▾

Open Workbooks using the Control Key

1. Click **File**, select ☞ Open _____, the Open dialog box appears

2. Double click with the left 🖱 button to open the required folder

3. Click the filename once with the left 🖱 button to select a workbook

4. Hold the CTRL key down, click with the left 🖱 button on the next workbook

5. Each selected file is highlighted in blue

6. If a file is selected by mistake click again to deselect

7. Click Open ▼ to open all the workbooks

Open Workbooks using the Shift Key

1. Click **File**, select ☞ Open

2. Double click with the left 🖱 button to open the required folder

3. Click the left 🖱 button to select the first workbook

4. Hold the SHIFT key down, click the left 🖱 button to select the last file

5. All selected files are highlighted in blue

6. Click Open ▼ to display all the workbooks

Introduction to Custom Lists

Why Use a Custom List?

If you need to repeat information on a regular basis, creating a Custom List is the best option.

Defining a Custom List

1. Click **File**, select ⬜ Options , Advanced

2. Using the left 🖱 button scroll down to the General area

3. Choose Edit Custom Lists...

4. The Custom Lists dialog box appears

Figure 15

5. The left hand side of the Custom lists dialog box displays the pre-set lists

6. To define a new custom list, click with the left 🖱 button in List entries area

7. Type out the list that you want to define

8. Press the Enter key after each list entry

9. When you have finished entering your list, select the Add icon

10. The list is added to the Custom lists area, press OK twice

Exercise 2: - Creating and Deleting a Custom List

The objective of this exercise is to define and reproduce information from a Custom List so that when the defined list has been created it can be reproduced in any worksheet.

Customer Services
Human Resources
Logistics
Payroll
Purchasing
Research and Development

1. Choose 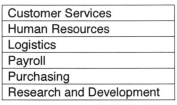 **File** , **Options** , **Advanced**

2. Scroll down and select **Edit Custom Lists...**

3. The left hand Custom lists dialog box displays the pre-set lists

4. To define a new custom list click the left 🖱 button in the List entries area

5. Type out the details shown above, each department should be on a different line

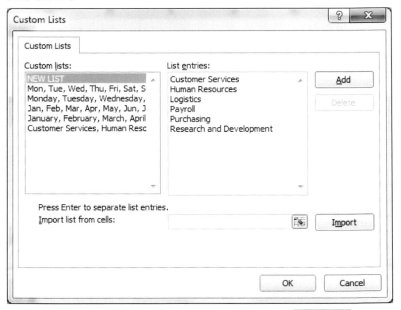

6. When you have finished entering your list select the **Add** icon

7. The list is added to the Custom lists area

8. Press **OK** twice

9. Click in a cell in any worksheet and type out Customer Services

10. Move the mouse pointer ⬉ over the bottom right hand corner

11. The white cross ⬦ changes to a thin black cross

12. Click with the left ⬦ button and drag down six cells

13. The information to be placed in the next cell appears [Human Resources]

14. Drag over the required cells then release the mouse

15. To Delete a custom list, choose [File], [⬦ Options],
    Advanced

16. Choose [Edit Custom Lists…], in the Custom list area select the list to be deleted

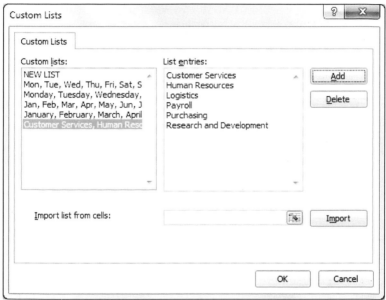

17. The list is highlighted, select [Delete]

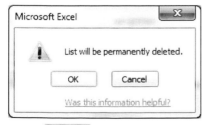

18. Press [OK], the list is deleted from the Custom Lists area

19. Select [OK] twice to return to the worksheet

Note: It is not possible to delete the pre-set custom lists.

Undo and Redo Facility

When entering information in a cell or a command is used, the information is stored in the memory. The Undo and Redo facility allows a user to go backwards or forwards on a step-by-step basis. The Undo and Redo icons are located on the Quick Access Toolbar located at the top left of the screen.

1. To undo an action click on the Undo icon

2. If you require to undo several steps, click on the downward arrow

3. Highlight over the steps that you want to undo

4. It is possible to go back a step if you have not saved the workbook

5. Repeat the same steps for the Redo icon

Note: **If you clicked on the downward arrow and selected the stage that you want to go back to, it will delete all the steps.**

Creating Simple Formula

In Excel 2010 the formula bar automatically resizes to accommodate long or complex formulas.

1. Create the following data

	A	B
1		
2		
3	**Regional Office**	**Sales**
4	Bath	26485
5	Birmingham	14000
6	Bristol	23675
7	Cardiff	34876
8	Manchester	8734
9	Nottingham	12398
10	Portsmouth	12876
11	Torquay	3421
12		
13	**Total**	

Figure 16

2. To add up the sales figures in column B

3. Select the cell where you want the answer to appear

4. All formula starts with equals ☐ = ☐ and the word sum

5. Type =sum, hold down the ☐ SHIFT ☐ key, press the opening bracket sign ☐ (☐

6. Once a bracket is open you can drag over the cells you want to add up

7. The cells are automatically referenced in the formula

8. Creating your formula in this way means less typing and fewer mistakes

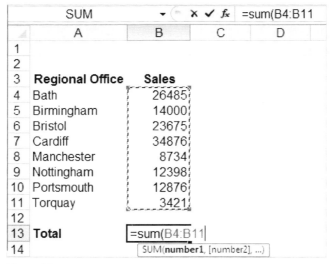

Figure 17

9. If you open a bracket you must close a bracket [ )]

10. Alternatively type =SUM(B4:B11) or
=SUM(B4+B5+B6+B7+B8+B9+B10+B11)

11. If you are using just one set of brackets and forget to close the bracket at the end of the formula, Excel will add this automatically

12. To complete the formula click on the blue tick ✓, or press [Enter]

13. The result displayed in cell B13 is 136465

14. Save the Workbook

AutoSum Icon

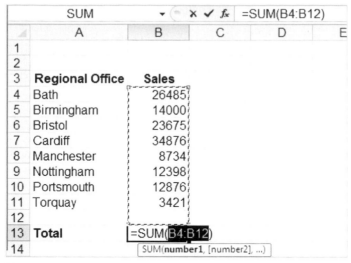

Figure 18

1. Select the Formulas Tab

2. Click in cell B13, select the AutoSum icon **Σ** from the Function Library Group

3. The formula appears =sum(B4:B12)

4. Cell B12 contains no information, however the AutoSum feature thinks you want to add up all the cells above B13

5. However, in this instance cell B12 **does not** want to be selected

6. A moving line appears around the area that Excel thinks you want to add up

7. Move the mouse pointer into the middle of cell B4

8. Click and hold down the left button, drag to cell B11

9. A line appears around the selected text, click on the blue tick ✓

10. Alternatively press the Enter key on the keyboard

11. B13 contains the result 136465

Note: If you required a formula that needed a blank line to separate the total from the data, create the formula result first then insert a row above the total.

Multiplication

	A	B	C	D
1		**Monthly Salary**	Tax	**Net Income**
2	Peter Bailey	£2,750.00		
3	Brian Carter	£1,670.00		
4	Kerry Jones	£945.00		
5	Sheila Mottram	£3,285.00		

Figure 19

The following steps display an easy way to create the multiplication formula. To multiply Excel uses the asterisk sign [*]. Remember all formula starts with the equals sign [=].

1. Create the above table, select cell C2, press [=]

2. Click in cell B2, the reference is displayed in the formula bar

3. Alternatively type out B2

4. Use the multiplication sign [*], type the TAX rate (in this instance 20%)

5. The correct formula is    SUM   ▾   × ✔ *fx*   =B2*20%

6. Click on the blue tick ✔ in the formula bar to remain in the cell

7. The information displayed in cell C2 should be £550.00

8. In cell C2, click on the black cross fill handle in the bottom right hand corner

       ┤← ———— Fill Handle

Figure 20

9. Drag over cells C3, C4 and C5

10. This formula is a relative reference; this means the formula is relative to each column and each row

C5		▾ (=	f_x =B5*20%	
	A	B	C	D
1		Monthly Salary	Tax	Net Income
2	Peter Bailey	£2,750.00	£550.00	
3	Brian Carter	£1,670.00	£334.00	
4	Kerry Jones	£945.00	£189.00	
5	Sheila Mottram	£3,285.00	£657.00	

Figure 21

11. The result appears in cells C3 to C5

Subtraction

	A	B	C	D
1		Monthly Salary	Tax	Net Income
2	Peter Bailey	£2,750.00	£550.00	
3	Brian Carter	£1,670.00	£334.00	
4	Kerry Jones	£945.00	£189.00	
5	Sheila Mottram	£3,285.00	£657.00	

Figure 22

1. All formula starts with the ⌷ = ⌷ sign

2. Click in cell D2, press ⌷ = ⌷ type B2-C2

3. Alternatively press the ⌷ = ⌷ sign, click in cell B2, press the ⌷ − ⌷ sign and click in cell C2

4. The cell reference is placed in the formula bar, press the ⌷ Enter ⌷ key

D2		▾ (=	f_x =B2-C2	
	A	B	C	D
1		Monthly Salary	Tax	Net Income
2	Peter Bailey	£2,750.00	£550.00	£2,200.00
3	Brian Carter	£1,670.00	£334.00	
4	Kerry Jones	£945.00	£189.00	
5	Sheila Mottram	£3,285.00	£657.00	

Figure 23

5. Move the mouse pointer ⬉ over the bottom right hand corner of D2

6. Click with the left ⬉ button on the black fill handle, drag down to cell D5

7. The results appear in cells D3 to D5

Division

Excel uses the forward slash key [/] to divide information.

	A	B	C	D
	D2	▾	f_x	
1		Amount Borrowed	Repayment Period	Monthly Cost
2	Car Loan	£4,500.00	48	
3	Car Loan	£21,500.00	36	
4	Car Loan	£13,750.00	24	
5	Car Loan	£11,250.00	12	

Figure 24

1. Create the following table
2. Select cell D2, press [=]
3. Click in cell B2 or type B2 in the formula bar, press [/]
4. Click in cell C2 or type C2, press [Enter]

D2	▾		f_x	=B2/C2

Figure 25

5. The result in cell D2 should be £93.75
6. Use the black fill handle to drag the results for D3, D4 and D5

Sum, Min, Max, Average, Count

Excel 2010 lets you quickly calculate statistical information, for example minimum, maximum, average and count. The function name used to add information together is **sum**.

	A	B	C	D	E
1		£25,678	£5,679	£25,762	£5,643
2		£87,905	£765	£86,257	£79,233
3		£567,900	£46,870	£67,543	£29,858
4		£76,549	£6,874	£26,718	£54,289
5		£79,567	£89,643	£79,567	£67,528
6					
7	Total	£837,599	£149,831	£285,847	£236,551
8	Min				
9	Max				
10	Average				
11	Count				

Figure 26

1. Select a new workbook, type out the information in Rows 1 - 5 shown above
2. Type the words in cells A7 to A11

3. Click with the left button in cell B7

4. Create the formula in cell B7, copy it across to cells C7, D7 and E7

5. Select cell B8, all formula starts with $=$

6. Instead of using the word Sum use the word Min

7. Insert the bracket sign $($

8. Click the left button in cell B1, a moving line appears around the cell

9. Hold the left button down and drag down to cell B5

SUM		× ✓ fx	=Min(B1:B5)	
	A	B	C	D	E
1		£25,678	£5,679	£25,762	£5,643
2		£87,905	£765	£86,257	£79,233
3		£567,900	£46,870	£67,543	£29,858
4		£76,549	£6,874	£26,718	£54,289
5		£79,567	£89,643	£79,567	£67,528
6					
7	Total	£837,599	£149,831	£285,847	£236,551
8	Min	=Min(B1:B5)			
9	Max				
10	Average				
11	Count				

Figure 27

10. The formula states =Min(B1:B5 in the cell and the formula bar

11. Close the bracket sign $)$

12. Click on the blue tick ✓ to remain in cell B8

13. Move the mouse pointer to the bottom right hand corner of cell B8

14. Use the black fill handle, click the left button and drag over C8 to E8

15. Release the left button, the formula is copied to the cells

16. Now create the formula for the Rows 9 to 11

	A	B	C	D	E
1		£25,678	£5,679	£25,762	£5,643
2		£87,905	£765	£86,257	£79,233
3		£567,900	£46,870	£67,543	£29,858
4		£76,549	£6,874	£26,718	£54,289
5		£79,567	£89,643	£79,567	£67,528
6					
7	Total	£837,599	£149,831	£285,847	£236,551
8	Min	£25,678	£765	£25,762	£5,643
9	Max	£567,900	£89,643	£86,257	£79,233
10	Average	£167,520	£29,966	£57,169	£47,310
11	Count	5	5	5	5

Figure 28

17. Save the workbook as Working with Total Min Max Average and Count

Insert Functions Feature

If a user was working in a workbook and forgot the function name of a formula, Excel provides a quick and easy access.

	A	B	C	D	E
1		£25,678	£5,679	£25,762	£5,643
2		£87,905	£765	£86,257	£79,233
3		£567,900	£46,870	£67,543	£29,858
4		£76,549	£6,874	£26,718	£54,289
5		£79,567	£89,643	£79,567	£67,528
6					
7	Total	£837,599	£149,831	£285,847	£236,551
8	Min	£25,678	£765	£25,762	£5,643
9	Max				
10	Average				
11	Count				

Figure 29

1. Using the above table, click on the Formulas Tab

2. Click with the left button in cell B9 where the results are to appear

3. Choose 𝑓𝑥 Insert Function from the Function Library Group

4. The Insert Function dialog box appears

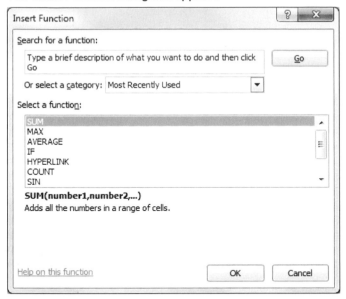

Figure 30

5. Under the heading **S**earch for a function, type max

6. Press [Go]

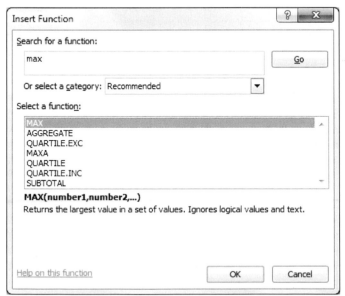

Figure 31

7. The description is displayed in the Select a function box

8. Click [OK], the Function Arguments dialog box appears

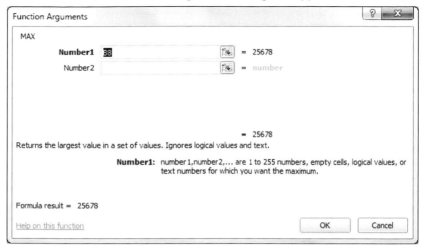

Figure 32

9. Select the dialog box icon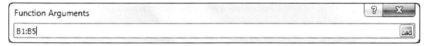

10. Click in the centre of cell B1 and drag to cell B5

11. =MAX(B1:B5) is displayed in the Formula Bar

12. The Functions Arguments dialog box displays the selected cells

Function Arguments	?	X
B1:B5		

Figure 33

13. Select the dialog box icon again

14. Click [OK] to display the results

Exercise 3: - Consolidation Working with Formulas

	A	B	C	D	E
1	**Name**	**Salary**	**Monthly**	**Tax**	**Total**
2	Wright	£16,570.00			
3	Broad	£57,000.00			
4	Parratt	£85,600.00			
5	Martin	£16,000.00			
6	Christian	£14,750.00			
7	Nichols	£17,800.00			
8	Layne	£16,870.00			
9	Kirby	£13,200.00			
10	Roberts	£22,000.00			
11	Davidson	£11,250.00			
12					
13	**Total**				
14	**Minimum**				
15	**Maximum**				
16	**Average**				
17	**Count**				

1. Open a new workbook
2. Create the information shown in columns A and E above
3. Click in cell B13, create a formula to calculate the total salary
4. Create individual formulas for cell B14 to B17
5. Select C2, create a formula to calculate the monthly salary
6. Use the fill handle to copy the relative formula to C11
7. Using a tax rate of 21.5% create a formula to display the monthly tax paid by each person
8. In column E work out the monthly take home pay for each person
9. Save the exercise as Working with Different Formulas

Moving Information

Moving information in Excel is easy, to move information in cell A6 to B2

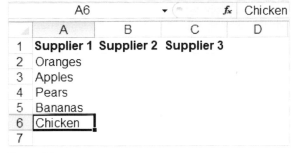

Figure 34

1. Type the above table in a new worksheet

2. Select cell A6, choose   Home   , click on the Cut icon   ✂ Cut

3. A moving dotted line appears around the selected cell

4. Click in cell B2, select the Paste icon

5. The information from cell A6 is moved to cell B2

Note: To use the right mouse button follow the same steps selecting the required icon.

Keyboard Shortcuts to Move Information

1. Select cell A6

2. Hold down the [CTRL] key, select [X]

3. A moving dotted line appears around the selected cell

4. Click in cell B2

5. Hold down the [CTRL] key, select [V]

6. The information from cell A6 is moved to cell B2

Drag and Drop Moving Information

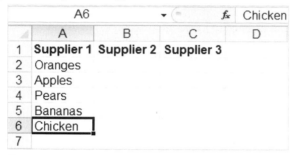

Figure 35

1. Select cell A6

2. Move the mouse pointer 𝕜 over the left hand corner of the cell A6

3. A pointing arrow appears

4. Click and hold down the left button

5. The left hand corner of the status bar states Drag to move cell contents

6. Keeping the left button down, drag to the new destination

7. Release the left button in cell B2

8. The information from cell A6 is moved to cell B2

Copying Information

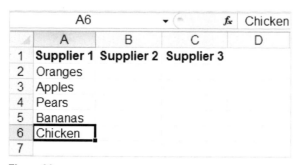

Figure 36

Copying information in cell A6 to B2

1. Select cell A6, press the Home Tab

2. Choose the Copy icon Copy

3. A moving dotted line appears around the selected cell

4. Click in cell B2, select the Paste icon

5. The information from cell A6 is copied in cell B2

6. The moving dotted line still appears around cell A6

7. To switch off the dotted line, press Enter or the ESC key on the keyboard

Keyboard Shortcuts to Copy Information

1. Select cell A6, hold down the CTRL key, select C

2. A moving dotted line appears around the selected cell

3. Click with your left button to select the new cell B2

4. Hold down the CTRL key and select V

5. The information from cell A6 is copied to cell B2

6. To switch off the dotted line, press Enter or the ESC key

Drag and Drop to Copy Information

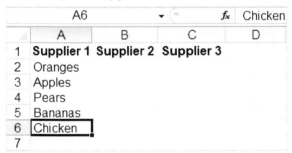

Figure 37

1. Select cell A6, move the mouse pointer over the left hand corner

2. Hold down the CTRL key and the left button

3. A plus sign + appears above the white arrow when the CTRL key is down

4. The bottom left hand corner of the Status Bar states Drag to copy cell contents

5. Drag with the mouse pointer to the new location

6. Release the left button before the CTRL key

7. The information in cell A6 has been copied to the new cell

BODMAS

What is BODMAS?

BODMAS is the mathematical method that Excel 2010 uses to calculate a formula.

Name	Description	Symbol
B	Brackets	( )
O	To The Power of	^
D	Division	/
M	Multiplication	*
A	Addition	+
S	Subtraction	–

Figure 38

Excel always uses the BODMAS rule to work out information in brackets before it completes the multiplication part of the formula.

To work out the answer to "what is 5+2*10?"

Using the BODMAS rule, Excel will work out the multiplication part of the formula before the 5+2, however if the formula is =(5+2)*10 then Excel will work out the information in brackets first and then multiply the result by 10.

Different Types of References

Reference	Description of Reference
$A$1	Defines always look at Column A and Row 1
A$1	Defines always look at Row 1 but not Column A
$A1	Defines always look at Column A but not Row 1
A1	This is a normal cell reference

Figure 39

Excel uses four different types of references when working with formula.   To change the reference

1. Select the cell that contains the formula
2. Click in the cell reference in the Formula Bar that needs to be changed
3. Press [F4] slowly four times
4. The reference goes through the four different cell reference options
5. Select the reference required
6. Alternatively type out the reference

Absolute Cell References

Absolute Cell Referencing saves time when working in Excel, for example if the VAT rate or a commission rate has been changed, Absolute Cell Referencing is a quick method of changing the reference that the formula is working to. The formula automatically updates information referenced in the cell.

	A	B	C	D
1	10%			
2		12500	16750	23000
3	Commission			

Figure 40

1. Type the above table in a new worksheet
2. Create the formula =B2*A1, Excel works out 10% of 12500
3. In a relative formula you could drag across using the fill handle and if applied the results would be cell C3 zero and cell D3 zero
4. That is because no absolute cell reference has been applied
5. (In the above example) absolute means "when applying the formula always look at cell A1"
6. To make a cell reference absolute use the following steps
7. Select cell B3
8. Click in the Formula Bar
9. After =B2*A1, a flashing cursor appears
10. Press ⌞F4⌟, dollar signs appear around A1

SUM		▾	✕ ✓ ƒ×	=B2*$A$1
	A	B	C	D
1	10%			
2		12500	16750	23000
3	Commission	=B2*$A$1		

Figure 41

11. Think of the dollar sign as saying "always look at Column A and always look at Row 1"
12. Select the blue tick ✓ to update the formula and remain in the cell
13. Use the fill handle to drag across C3 and D3
14. The formula in cell C3 is =C2*$A$1
15. The formula in cell D3 is =D2*$A$1

Formatting Options

Formatting is a quick way to apply different layouts or designs to your worksheet. In Excel 2010, the Ribbon has seven Tabs; each tab groups together related items that enable the user to carry out a series of commands.

The Font Group Icons

Icon	Descriptive Prompt
Arial	Font Face
12	Font Size
A˄	Increase Font Size
A˅	Decrease Font Size
B	**Makes selected text and numbers bold**
I	*Makes selected text and numbers italic*
U	Makes selected text and numbers underlined
D	Makes selected text and numbers double underlined
	Borders
	Fill Colour
A	Font Colour
	Click the left button to open the Format Cells dialog box

Figure 42

Formatting Cells using the Font Group

1. Select the Home Tab to display the Font Group

Figure 43

2. Select the cells that require formatting

3. Change the font by clicking on the Font Face icon Arial

4. A drop down menu displaying the Theme Fonts appears

5. Change the name of the font to Arial or a font of your choice

6. Click on the Font Size icon 12 , change the font size

7. Alternatively press CTRL SHIFT F on the keyboard to display the Format Cells dialog box

The Alignment Group Icons

Icon	Descriptive Prompt
≡	Top Align
≡	Middle Align
≡	Bottom Align
⁇	Orientation rotate text
≡	Aligns the selected text, numbers, or objects to the left
≡	Centres the selected text, numbers, or objects
≡	Aligns the selected text, numbers, or objects to the right
⁝	Decrease Indent
⁝	Increase Indent
Wrap Text	Wrap Text
Merge & Center ▾	Merge and Centre
Merge Across	Merge Across
Merge Cells	Merge Cells
Unmerge Cells	Unmerge Cells
⌐	Click the left 🖰 button to open the Format Cells dialog box

Figure 44

Formatting Cells using the Alignment Group

1. Select the `Home` Tab to display the Alignment Group

Figure 45

2. Select the cells that require formatting
3. Change the alignment by clicking on the Align Text Command icon ≡
4. Alternatively press ⌊CTRL⌋ ⌊SHIFT⌋ ⌊ F ⌋ ⌊ A ⌋ on the keyboard to display the Alignment Tab in the Format Cells dialog box

The Number Group Icons

Icon	Descriptive Prompt
General ▾	Number Format
🖩 ▾	Accounting Number Format
%	Percentage Style
,	Comma Style
⁺.0/.00	Increase Decimal
.00/⁺.0	Decrease Decimal
▵	Use the left 🖱 button to open the Format Cells dialog box

Figure 46

Formatting Cells using the Number Group

1. Select the Home Tab to display the Number Group

Figure 47

2. Select the cells that require formatting

3. Change the numbering by clicking on the Comma Style icon ,

4. Alternatively press ⌨ CTRL ⌨ SHIFT ⌨ F ⌨ N on the keyboard to display the Number Tab in the Format Cells dialog box

Borders

The Borders icon adds or removes borders around selected cells. To display the different types of borders

1. Highlight the cells that require a border

2. Select   Home

3. Click on the More Borders icon ⊞ ˅ in the Font Group

4. The Borders menu appears

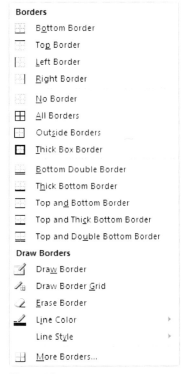

Figure 48

5. Choose ⊞ More Borders...

6. The Format Cells dialog box appears with the Border Tab selected

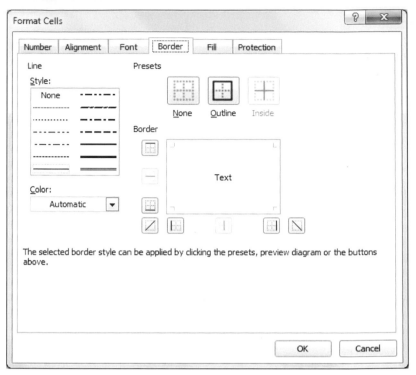

Figure 49

7. Choose the **S**tyle of line and **C**olour required

8. Select **O**utline or Inside border

9. Click on the [Fill] Tab

10. Select Background **C**olour and choose the colour required

11. Click [OK]

12. To remove a border, highlight the cells

13. Click on the More Borders icon

14. Select No Border

15. To remove the fill colour, highlight the cells

16. Click on the Fill Colour icon

17. Select No Fill

Home Tab

When using Excel 2010, it is possible to format a worksheet using the Home Tab and by selecting the cells to be changed. You must select the cell(s) before you can format information.

1. Highlight the cells to be formatted

2. Select   Home

Format

3. Choose   ˅   from the Cells Grouping

4. The Cell Size menu appears

5. Select Format Cells...

6. The Format Cells dialog box appears

7. Click on the Number Tab

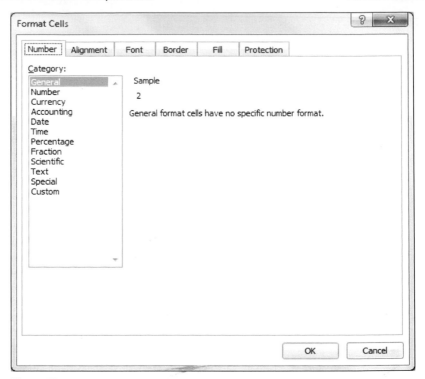

Figure 51

8. Select **C**ategory and choose the required format

9. Click <u>OK</u>

Align Information using the Home Tab

1. Highlight the cells to be formatted

2. Select Home

   Format

3. Choose ˅ from the Cells Grouping

4. Select 🔺 Format Cells...

5. Click on the Alignment Tab

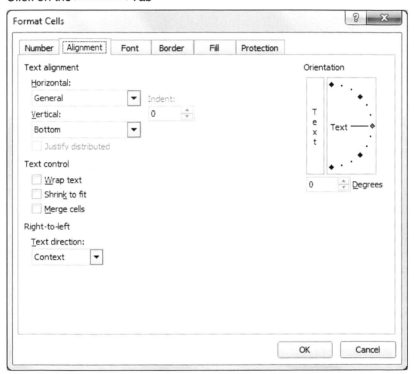

Figure 52

6. Change the **H**orizontal and **V**ertical options to Centre

7. Orientation enables 'text' information to be displayed at an angle

8. Change the Text control to either **W**rap text, Shrin**k** to fit or **M**erge cells

9. Click OK

Formatting Text

1. Highlight the cells to be formatted

2. Select `Home` , choose `Format ▾` , `Format Cells...`

3. Click on the `Font` Tab

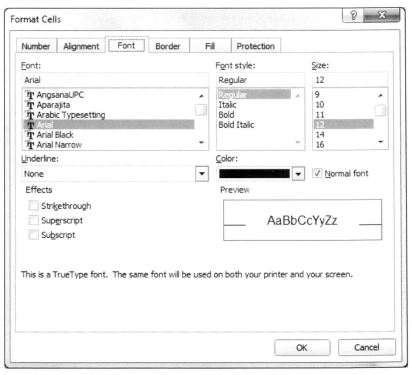

Figure 53

4. Choose Font and select the type of font required

5. Repeat these steps to change the Font style, Size, Underline and Colour

6. Strikethrough, Superscript and Subscript are special alignment options

7. The selected formatting options are displayed in the Preview area

8. Click `OK` to apply the changes

Fill Tab

The [Fill] Tab sets the background colour of a highlighted area.

1. To format cells using the [Fill] Tab, select the cells to be formatted

2. Select Home , choose Format ▾ , 🖉 Format Cells...

3. The Format Cells dialog box appears

4. Click on the [Fill] Tab

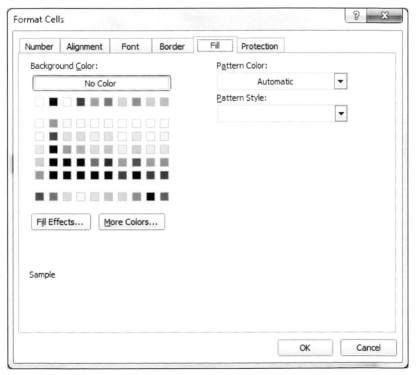

Figure 54

5. Choose Background **C**olour, select the background colour from the menu

6. Follow the same steps to select a **Pa**ttern Colour and/or a **P**attern Style

7. The selection can be seen in the Sample area

8. Click [OK] to apply the changes

Format Painter Icon

Using the Format Painter icon *Format Painter* allows users to copy formatting from one place and apply it to another.

1. Click in the cell with the format you want to copy

2. Select Home , move the mouse pointer ⏰ to *Format Painter*

3. Double click the *Format Painter* to apply the format to multiple cells

4. When the Format Painter icon is switched on it is indented

5. When moving over the cell you will see a white cross and brush

6. A dotted line appears around the original cell

7. Click with the left 🖱 button in the cell you want to apply the format

8. The format of the cell is changed to that of the original cell

9. Switch the Format Painter off by selecting the icon again

10. The dotted line disappears when the facility is switched off

11. To apply a format to one cell

12. Select *Format Painter* once

13. When the cell is selected the Format Painter automatically switches itself off

Page Layout Tab

The Page Setup Grouping includes quick and easy commands that allow changes to be made to margins, orientation, size, print area, breaks, background and print titles.

1. Select the Page Layout Tab, the Page Setup grouping is displayed

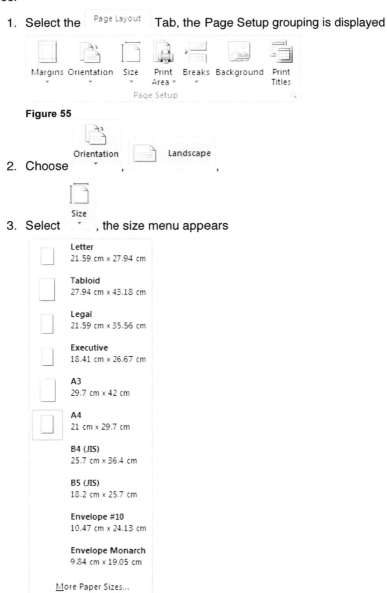

Figure 55

2. Choose Orientation , Landscape ,

3. Select Size , the size menu appears

Letter
21.59 cm x 27.94 cm

Tabloid
27.94 cm x 43.18 cm

Legal
21.59 cm x 35.56 cm

Executive
18.41 cm x 26.67 cm

A3
29.7 cm x 42 cm

A4
21 cm x 29.7 cm

B4 (JIS)
25.7 cm x 36.4 cm

B5 (JIS)
18.2 cm x 25.7 cm

Envelope #10
10.47 cm x 24.13 cm

Envelope Monarch
9.84 cm x 19.05 cm

More Paper Sizes...

Figure 56

4. Select the required paper size

5. Select **File**, **Print** to preview the worksheet

6. Or press CTRL F2

7. Press the ESC key on the keyboard to return to the worksheet

8. Alternatively click with the left 🖱 button on the Page Setup dialog box launcher 🔲

9. The Page Setup dialog box appears

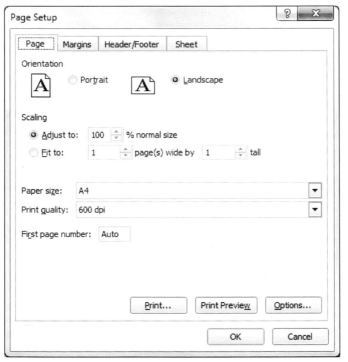

Figure 57

10. Select the required options, click OK

Margins

1. Using the Page Layout Tab, select 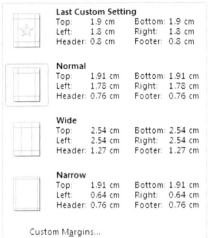, the margins menu is displayed

Figure 58

2. Change the margins by selecting Normal, Wide or Narrow

3. Or press Custom Margins... , the Page Setup dialog box appears

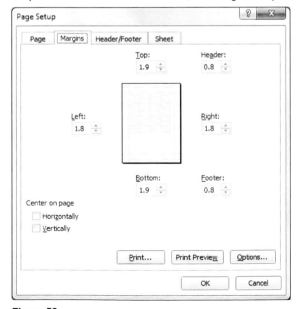

Figure 59

4. Select the Margins Tab
5. Change the default settings Top, Bottom, Left and Right
6. Click on the Horizontally and Vertically options to centre on the page
7. The Header and Footer margins can also be changed from this screen
8. Click OK

Headers and Footers

1. Select Page Layout , Margins, the margins menu is displayed
2. Choose Custom Margins..., the Page Setup dialog box appears
3. Select the Header/Footer Tab

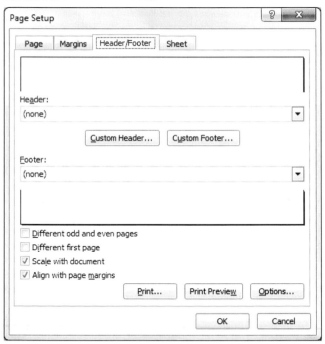

Figure 60

4. The Header and Footer boxes provide a preview of both areas

Figure 61

5. Choose the downward pointing arrows to view the standard pre-set options

6. The preview area displays the selected option

7. Click on the downward pointing arrow to return to the Header/Footer Tab

8. To create a Custom Header, select Custom Header...

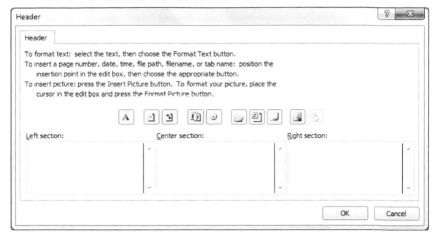

Figure 62

9. The Header and Footer icons are shown below

Header and Footer Options	
Icon	**Descriptive Prompt**
A	Define font size and style options
#]	Inserts the Page Number
+]	Inserts Number of Pages
{7]	Insert Date
⊙	Insert Time
📁	Insert File Path
📄]	Insert File Name
⌐	Insert Sheet Name
🖼	Insert Picture
⅋	Format Picture
OK	Accept Changes and go back to Page Setup options
Cancel	Go back to the Page Set Up Options

Figure 63

10. Create the Header and Footer information, click [OK]

11. The [Custom Footer...] icon enables the Footer area to be created

12. Create the Footer information, click [OK] twice

13. To preview the Header and Footer information press [CTRL] [F2]

Exercise 4: - Creating Header and Footer Information

1. Open the workbook named Working with Different Formulas
2. Create a centre heading using the name of a school or organisation
3. Select the Custom Footer, in the Centre section create Page 1 of 1
4. Preview your worksheet to view the changes
5. Save the Workbook

Define a Print Area

1. Using the Page Layout Tab, select Print Titles

2. Or click on the Page Setup dialog box launcher

3. Select the Sheet Tab, click on the Print <u>a</u>rea icon

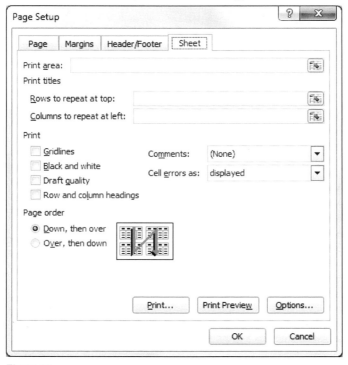

Figure 64

4. The Page Setup Print area: box is displayed

Figure 65

5. Highlight the cells, the absolute references will appear in the print area

6. A dotted line appears around the selected area

7. Click on the Print area icon to close the Print area window

8. Select Print Preview , choose Print

Clear a Print Area

1. Select the [Page Layout] Tab

2. Click on the Print Area icon [Area ▾]

3. Select [Clear Print Area]

Note: **If a print area is defined and a further area needs to be selected; select the additional area and click the print area icon. Select add to print area icon to update the print area selection.**

Print Preview

1. Select [File], [Print] to preview the worksheet

2. Alternatively press [CTRL] [F2]

3. Click with the left ⬚ button on the zoom to page icon in the bottom right corner of the screen

4. Use the left ⬚ button to move the vertical/horizontal scroll bars to view data

5. Click with the left ⬚ button on the zoom to page icon to zoom out

6. For more than one page use the next page icon ▶

7. Press the previous page icon to go back a page ◀

8. The current page and total number of pages are displayed ◀ 1 of 2 ▶ below the preview area

9. Click on the Show Margins icon to display or adjust the margins

10. Move the mouse pointer over the margin to be adjusted ┳ or ┣

11. The mouse pointer changes to the following sign ╬

12. Click and drag with the left ⬚ button to increase or decrease the margin

13. Release the left ⬚ button once the new margin has been set

14. Press the [ESC] key on the keyboard to return to the spreadsheet

Printing

1. Select **File**, **Print**

2. The Backstage view displays Print Preview and the Print dialog box

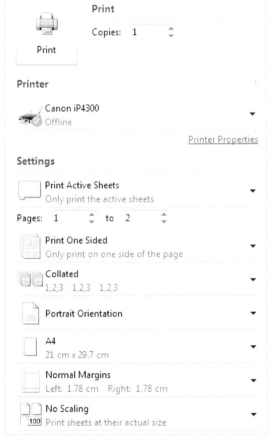

Figure 66

3. Choose the Number of copies required, default is 1 copy

4. In the Printer area, the active printer is shown

5. To change the printer click on the downward arrow to select the required printer

6. Select the Settings required by clicking on the appropriate downward pointing arrows

7. Select Print Active Sheets to print only the active sheets

8. Select Print One Sided to print on one side of the page

9. Choose Collate to collate the worksheets

10. Choose the required Orientation, select the required paper size

11. Set the margins required, choose scaling if required

12. Any changes made to the worksheet appear in the print preview window

Print

13. Select

14. Alternatively  displays the Print dialog box

Spell Feature

The Spell Feature checks the text in a workbook for incorrect spelling using the standard built in dictionary that can also be customised.

ABC
Spelling

1. Select   Review   , choose   , or press   F7

2. The spelling dialog box appears if there are spelling errors in the text

Figure 67

Figure 68

3. Press   OK   to return to the worksheet

Introduction to Simple Charts

Excel 2010 allows the user to create a chart from information that the user has been working with and displays this data graphically in an embedded chart that can be placed and saved on the same sheet as your data, or on a chart sheet that displays the data separately from the data sheet. Both the embedded chart and the chart sheet are automatically updated when data on the worksheet is changed.

Different Parts of a Chart

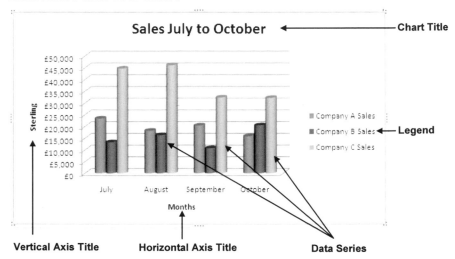

Figure 69

Chart Title

The chart title identifies the name of the chart.

Legend

The Legend defines the symbols used in each data series in the chart.

Vertical Y Axis

Indicates the unit of measurement used in the chart.

Horizontal X Axis

Indicates the categories used in the chart.

Data Series

The Data Series represents a group of data incorporated in a row or column from an Excel worksheet. A chart consists of one or more data series.

A chart can be resized using the mouse by dragging from any of the corner points of the chart.

Creating a Simple Chart

1. Create the following table

	A	B	C	D	E	F
1		April	May	June	July	Total
2	Company A	£23,400	£18,200	£20,421	£15,876	£77,897
3	Company B	£13,275	£16,320	£10,745	£20,486	£60,826
4	Company C	£44,739	£46,100	£32,400	£30,200	£153,439

Figure 70

2. Select cells A1 to E4 using the left 🖱 button

3. Choose the Insert Tab

Column

4. Select the ▼ icon from the Charts Grouping

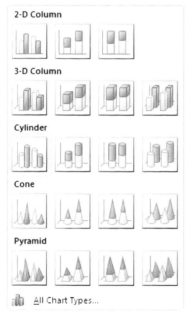

Figure 71

5. Select Clustered Cylinder

6. The chart appears on the worksheet as shown below

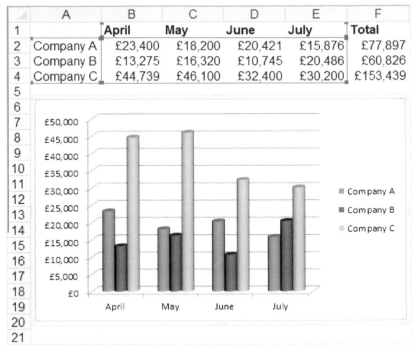

	A	B	C	D	E	F
1		April	May	June	July	Total
2	Company A	£23,400	£18,200	£20,421	£15,876	£77,897
3	Company B	£13,275	£16,320	£10,745	£20,486	£60,826
4	Company C	£44,739	£46,100	£32,400	£30,200	£153,439

Figure 72

7. To add, remove or update data in the chart

8. Click in the cell where information is to be added, removed or updated

9. Type in the changes, press the Enter key

10. The chart is updated automatically

11. To add a heading, legend, category and value data to the chart

12. Click with the left button in the chart area to activate the chart tools

13. The Chart Tools are highlighted   Design   Layout   Format

14. Choose the Design Tab

15. Select the Chart Layouts Grouping

Figure 73

16. Use the downward pointing arrow  to expand the menu box

17. Choose Layout 9

Figure 74

18. Click on Chart Title in the chart

19. Change the title to Sales April to July, click outside the Chart Title area

20. Click on the horizontal axis title, type Months, click outside the Horizontal Axis Title area

21. Type Sterling in the vertical axis box

Figure 75

22. Save the chart as My Simple Chart

Adding New Data to a Chart

1. Select the original worksheet My Simple Chart

2. To add the figures for August

Insert

3. Click in cell F2 select   Home   Tab, click   ▾   from the Cells Grouping

4. Choose ¦↓ Insert Sheet Columns , the new column is inserted

5. Click in cell F1 type August as the heading

6. In cell F2 type £16,000

7. In cell F3 type £25,125

8. In cell F4 type £31,965

9. Change the chart title to Sales April to August

10. Click in the Chart Area, a blue border appears around the figures April to July

	A	B	C	D	E	F	G
1		April	May	June	July	August	Total
2	Company A	£23,400	£18,200	£20,421	£15,876	£16,000	£93,897
3	Company B	£13,275	£16,320	£10,745	£20,486	£25,125	£85,951
4	Company C	£44,739	£46,100	£32,400	£30,200	£31,965	£185,404

Figure 76

11. Move the mouse pointer 🔍 on the blue square ◢ in column E

12. Click with the left 🖱 button and drag to include the figures for August

13. The chart is updated automatically as displayed on the next page

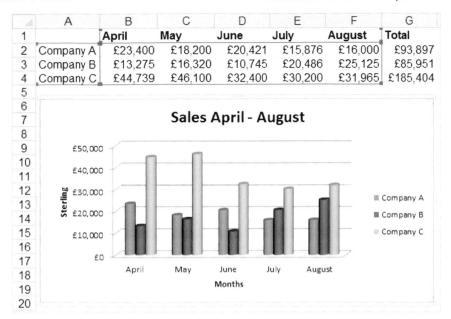

	A	B	C	D	E	F	G
1		April	May	June	July	August	Total
2	Company A	£23,400	£18,200	£20,421	£15,876	£16,000	£93,897
3	Company B	£13,275	£16,320	£10,745	£20,486	£25,125	£85,951
4	Company C	£44,739	£46,100	£32,400	£30,200	£31,965	£185,404

Figure 77

Changing the Style of a Chart

1. Click in the chart, select the Design Tab, choose chart styles

2. Select the style required by using the downward pointing arrow

3. The chart is updated automatically

Figure 78

Changing the Type of Chart

1. Click in the chart, select [Design], [Change Chart Type] in the Type Groupings
2. The Change Chart Type dialog box appears

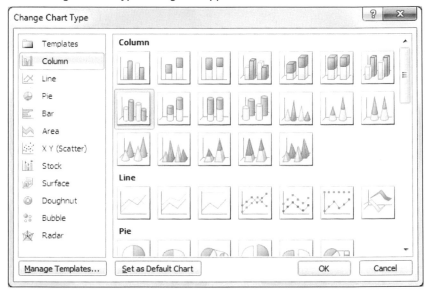

Figure 79

3. Select the chart type required, press [OK]

Figure 80

Printing a Chart Sheet

1. Click with the left button on any area of the chart

2. Select **File**, **Print**

3. Choose Page Setup at the bottom right hand corner of the print dialog box

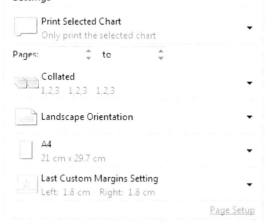

Figure 81

4. Select the Header/Footer Tab

5. Create a Custom Header... and Custom Footer...

Print

6. Click OK , select

7. Save the workbook

Exercise 5: - Create a Chart within a Worksheet

Using the data in the previous section update the chart as follows:

1. Change the chart title to read Company Sales April to September
2. Add the September figures as follows:
3. Company A £25,568
4. Company B £30,765
5. Company C £34,236
6. Update the Totals
7. Print the chart to include the figures for April to September
8. Save the workbook

Section 2

Intermediate Level Objectives

Naming a Worksheet and Navigation

Excel opens three worksheets in a workbook by default. To open more worksheets:

1. Click **File**, select  Options, General

2. The Excel Options dialog appears

When creating new workbooks	
Use this font:	Arial
Font size:	12
Default view for new sheets:	Normal View
Include this many sheets:	5

Figure 82

3. Choose the option: When creating new workbooks

4. Select: Include this many **s**heets

5. Type in the number of sheets required or use the arrow keys

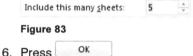
Include this many sheets: 5

Figure 83

6. Press OK

7. To display the new default number of worksheets

8. Click **File**, select **New**, Create

9. The new default worksheets appear

Inserting Worksheets

1. Open a new workbook to bring up the 5 sheets

Sheet1 / Sheet2 / Sheet3 / Sheet4 / Sheet5

Figure 84

2. Click on the Insert Worksheet icon

3. The new active sheet appears to the right of the previously selected sheet

Sheet5   Sheet6

Figure 85

4. To delete a worksheet
5. Click with the right button over the worksheet to be deleted

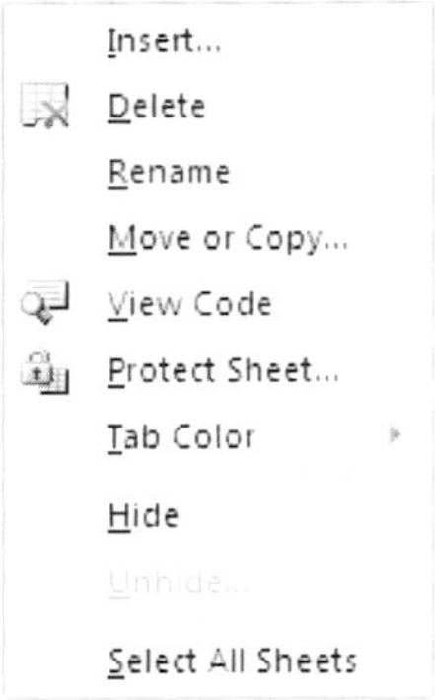
Insert...
Delete
Rename
Move or Copy...
View Code
Protect Sheet...
Tab Color
Hide
Unhide...
Select All Sheets

Figure 86

6. Select Delete

View Unseen Worksheets

If worksheets are not displayed

1. Select the icon with the left button to display Sheet 1
2. Choose the icon to display the last sheet in the workbook
3. Click the icons to display the concealed worksheets

View Sheet Tabs

1. Using the horizontal scroll bar

Figure 87

2. Move the mouse pointer over the left hand side of the arrow
3. A black vertical double line appears with arrows each side of the lines
4. Click and hold down the left button and drag to the right
5. The concealed worksheets are displayed

Rename a Worksheet

1. Double click with the left button on Sheet 1
2. The sheet name is highlighted Sheet1
3. Type the new name for the sheet, maximum of 31 characters

Rename a Worksheet using the Right Mouse Button

1. Move the white arrow over Sheet 2

Figure 88

2. Press the right ⟨mouse⟩ button, select Rename
3. The sheet is highlighted Sheet2
4. Rename the sheet, the new name is displayed

Move a Worksheet

1. Click and hold down the left ⟨mouse⟩ button on Sheet 1

   ⏮ ◀ ▶ ⏭ Sheet1 Sheet2 Sheet3 Sheet4 Sheet5

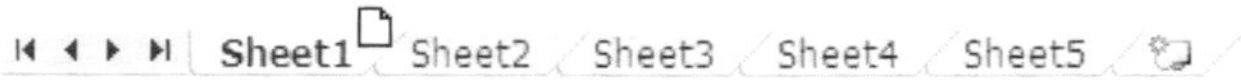

   Figure 89

2. A downward pointing black arrow appears on the sheet tab

3. Hold down the left ⟨mouse⟩ button, use the arrow as a guide

4. This displays where the new sheet will be positioned

5. Drag Sheet 1 to its new position after Sheet 3

6. Let go of the left ⟨mouse⟩ button, the sheet has moved to its new position

7. Move Sheet 1 back to its original position

Move or Copy a Worksheet

1. Select the sheet tab to be moved or copied using the left button

2. Click with the right button, select Move or Copy...

3. The Move or Copy dialog box appears

Figure 90

4. Choose the location where the selected sheet needs to be moved to

5. To create a copy, click with the left button on ☑ Create a copy

6. Click OK

Note: **To move or copy a new workbook or an active workbook that is opened select the ▼ arrow in the To book: area.**

Applying Colours to Worksheet Tabs

1. Select a sheet tab to apply a colour

2. Click with the right ⬤ button, choose Tab Color ▸

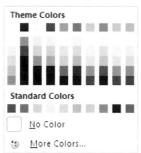

Figure 91

3. Select the required colour

4. Select a different tab, the new colour Sheet3 is displayed

Multiple Worksheets

Excel allows a number of sheets to be selected using the left ⬤ button. If you are creating a number of sheets using the same headings, highlight the sheets concerned, type the headings. The formatting will be applied to all the selected sheets.

1. Click on the tab named Sheet 1

2. Hold down the CTRL key and click on Sheet 3 and Sheet 5

3. [Group] appears in the title bar at the top of the screen

4. The word group identifies that more than one sheet has been selected

5. Type Smart PC Guides in cell A1

6. Widen column A

7. To deselect the group

8. Click with the right ⬤ button on any sheet tab

9. Select Ungroup Sheets

10. The group name disappears

11. Smart PC Guides appears on Sheets 3 and 5

Note: To select a group of sheets next to each other, click on the first sheet, select SHIFT before clicking on the last sheet. All the sheets are selected and the Title Bar displays the Group option.

Deleting Worksheets

1. Click with the right 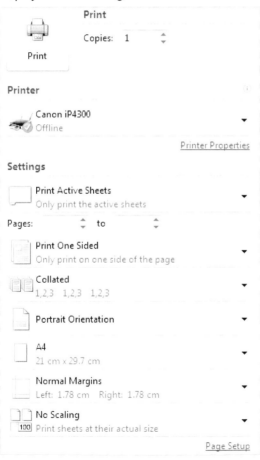 button over the sheet tab to be deleted
2. Select ⬚ Delete
3. The sheet is deleted from the workbook

Printing Multiple Worksheets

1. Select the sheets that require printing
2. The [Group] selection is displayed in the Title Bar
3. Select File, Print to preview the worksheets and display the Print dialog box

Print

Copies: 1

Print

Printer

Canon iP4300
Offline

Printer Properties

Settings

Print Active Sheets
Only print the active sheets

Pages: to

Print One Sided
Only print on one side of the page

Collated
1,2,3   1,2,3   1,2,3

Portrait Orientation

A4
21 cm x 29.7 cm

Normal Margins
Left: 1.78 cm   Right: 1.78 cm

No Scaling
100 Print sheets at their actual size

Page Setup

Figure 92

4. In the Settings area **Print Active Sheets** — Only print the active sheets — is selected

5. Click with the left button on the zoom to page icon in the bottom right corner of the screen

6. The vertical/horizontal scroll bars enable the data to be viewed

7. Click with the left button on the zoom to page icon to zoom out

8. For more than one page use the next page icon ▶

9. Press the previous page icon to go back a page ◀

10. The current page and total number of pages are displayed ◀ 1 of 5 ▶ below the preview area

11. Click on the Show Margins icon to display or adjust the margins

12. Move the mouse pointer over the margin to be adjusted ┳ or ┣

13. The mouse pointer changes to the following sign ╬

14. Click and drag with the left button to increase or decrease the margin

15. Release the left button once the new margin has been set

16. Select

Exercise 6: - Working with Multiple Sheets

1. Choose **File**, select New, choose Blank Workbook

2. Select Create

3. Rename four worksheets Qtr 1, Qtr 2, Qtr 3, Qtr 4

4. Group Sheets Qtr 1 to Qtr 4

5. Create the information below

	A	B	C	D	E	F
1		North	South	East	West	Total
2	Company 1					£0
3	Company 2					£0
4	Company 3					£0
5	Company 4					£0
6						
7	Total		£0	£0	£0	£0

6. Format cells B2:F5 to Currency

7. Format B7:E7 to Currency

8. Use AutoSum to create the totals

9. Ungroup all the sheets

10. Select the sheet named Qtr 1

11. Create a copy of Qtr 1, rename the sheet Consolidation

12. In Qtr 1 type the following data

	A	B	C	D	E	F
1		North	South	East	West	Total
2	Company 1	£14,000	£86,000	£74,000	£89,000	£263,000
3	Company 2	£73,000	£89,000	£55,000	£23,000	£240,000
4	Company 3	£46,000	£29,000	£67,000	£15,000	£157,000
5	Company 4	£8,000	£43,000	£23,000	£18,000	£92,000
6						
7	Total		£141,000	£247,000	£219,000	£145,000

13. In Qtr 2 type the following data

	A	B	C	D	E	F
1		North	South	East	West	Total
2	Company 1	£14,000	£7,000	£21,000	£20,000	£62,000
3	Company 2	£23,000	£11,000	£12,000	£10,000	£56,000
4	Company 3	£22,000	£46,000	£46,000	£46,000	£160,000
5	Company 4	£8,000	£8,000	£8,000	£8,000	£32,000
6						
7	Total		£67,000	£72,000	£87,000	£84,000

14. In Qtr 3 type the following data

	A	B	C	D	E	F
1		North	South	East	West	Total
2	Company 1	£120,000	£86,000	£43,000	£28,000	£277,000
3	Company 2	£23,000	£132,000	£54,000	£45,000	£254,000
4	Company 3	£46,000	£120,000	£12,000	£33,000	£211,000
5	Company 4	£32,000	£8,000	£8,000	£8,000	£56,000
6						
7	Total		£221,000	£346,000	£117,000	£114,000

15. Type the following data for Qtr 4

	A	B	C	D	E	F
1		North	South	East	West	Total
2	Company 1	£14,000	£14,000	£76,000	£14,000	£118,000
3	Company 2	£23,000	£122,000	£23,000	£23,000	£191,000
4	Company 3	£46,000	£18,000	£32,000	£63,000	£159,000
5	Company 4	£38,000	£12,000	£56,000	£83,000	£189,000
6						
7	Total		£121,000	£166,000	£187,000	£183,000

16. Save the workbook as Working with Multiple Sheets

3 Dimensional Formula

To analyse data in the same cell or range of cells on multiple worksheets, it is possible to create a 3D formula.

1. Open the workbook Working with Multiple Sheets

2. Select the Consolidation worksheet and click on cell B2

3. To create a 3D formula Type =sum(

4. Click on worksheet Quarter 1

5. Hold the SHIFT key down, select worksheet Quarter 4

6. Select cell B2

7. The formula is displayed in the formula bar =sum('Qtr 1:Qtr 4'!B2)

8. Click on the blue tick ✓ to confirm the formula

9. The result is displayed in cell B2 in the Consolidation Worksheet

10. Use the black cross fill handle to drag down to cell E5

11. The formula has added up the data in cell B2 in each quarter

12. Save the workbook

Note: If a worksheet is moved or inserted into a workbook that contains a 3D formula, the formula incorporates the figures in the results of the formula. The opposite is true if a sheet was part of a 3D formula and the sheet was moved or deleted.

Window Panes

Excel can freeze a column that will enable the heading rows to be seen at all times as the user scrolls across a worksheet.

Freezing the Left Pane

1. Open the workbook Working with Multiple Sheets

2. Choose the worksheet named Quarter 4

3. Select cell B2

4. Click on   View   , select   Freeze Panes ▾   from the Window Grouping

5. The following menu appears

Figure 93

6. Select <u>F</u>reeze Panes

7. Black indicator lines appear both to the left and above cell B2

8. Use the ⟶ key to move along the row

9. The heading rows are visible as you move to cell Z2

10. To move back a cell use the ⟵ key

11. Freeze panes ensures both column and row headings are visible

12. To unfreeze panes

13. Choose   Freeze Panes ▾ , select

Note: Using Freeze Panes does not change or affect the printing of a worksheet.

Freezing the Top Row

1. Select cell A2, the row below the Column Headings

Freeze

2. Click on View , select Panes ▾ from the Window Grouping

3. The following menu appears

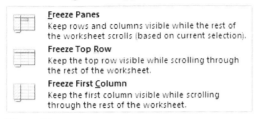

Freeze Panes
Keep rows and columns visible while the rest of
the worksheet scrolls (based on current selection).

Freeze Top Row
Keep the top row visible while scrolling through
the rest of the worksheet.

Freeze First Column
Keep the first column visible while scrolling
through the rest of the worksheet.

Figure 94

4. Select Freeze Top Row

5. A horizontal freeze pane line appears

6. Use the ⬇ key to go to cell A75, all the column headings remain

7. Unfreeze the pane

Splitting a Window View

Splitting a window enables a user to view different areas of a large worksheet at the same time. The screen can be split into four different sections.

1. Click in cell B2

2. Select View , choose Split from the Window Grouping

3. The screen splits into four sections

4. To move a split window

5. Move the mouse pointer over the split line

6. Press and hold down the left button, drag to the required position

7. To remove the split screen select Split

Working with Different Chart Types

Using different charts means that information can be easily understood by evaluating data and making it more interesting to read; charts can be used to help analyse and compare data.

3-D Bar Stacked Chart

1. Create the following information below

	A	B	C	D	E	F
1		July	August	September	October	Total
2	**Resort West**	£23,000	£18,200	£20,421	£18,876	£80,497
3	**Resort North**	£13,275	£16,320	£20,745	£20,486	£70,826
4	**Resort South**	£44,739	£46,100	£32,400	£30,200	£153,439

Figure 95

2. Save the worksheet as Working with Charts

3. Highlight cells A1:D4, select Insert

4. Choose from the Charts Grouping

5. The charts menu appears, select Stacked Bar in 3-D

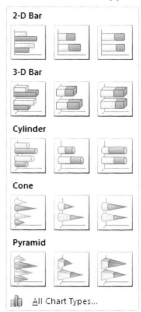

Figure 96

6. Select the Design Tab

Switch
7. Click on Row/Column from the Data Grouping

8. The layout of the Horizontal and Vertical axis changes

9. The selected area for the chart is displayed on the worksheet

	A	B	C	D	E	F
1		July	August	September	October	Total
2	**Resort West**	£23,000	£18,200	£20,421	£18,876	£80,497
3	**Resort North**	£13,275	£16,320	£20,745	£20,486	£70,826
4	**Resort South**	£44,739	£46,100	£32,400	£30,200	£153,439

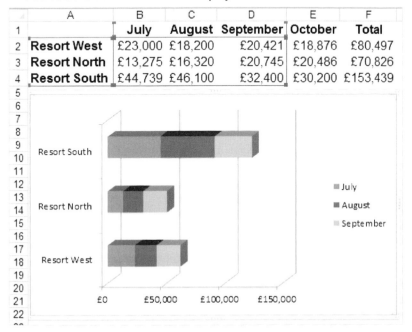

Figure 97

Customising a Chart

To remove or update data in the chart:

23. Click in the cell where information is to be removed or updated

24. Type in the changes, the chart is updated automatically

25. To add data to the chart

26. Click with the left ⬚ button in the chart area to activate the chart tools

27. Choose Design , select the Chart Layouts Grouping

28. Use the downward pointing arrow ⤓ to expand the menu box

29. Choose Layout 7

Figure 98

30. Click on the Horizontal Axis Title, type Sales

31. Click on the Vertical Axis Title, type Location

32. Click anywhere in the chart to display the titles

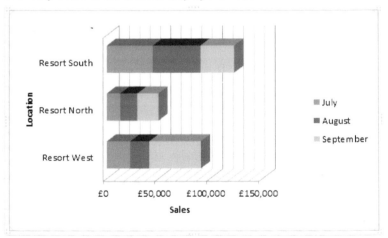

Figure 99

Adding New Data to a Chart

14. Click anywhere in the chart with the right 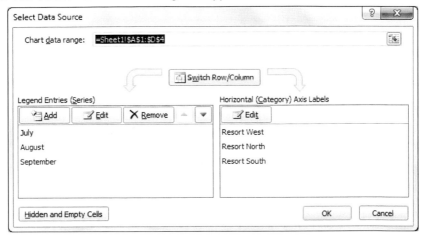 button

15. Choose ⬛ S_elect Data...   from the menu

16. The Select Data Source dialog box appears

Figure 100

17. Click [⬛ _Add], the Edit Series dialog box appears

Figure 101

18. Press the Series **n**ame icon 🔳, select October

19. Click 🔳 to return to the Edit Series dialog box

20. Click on the Series **v**alues icon 🔳, highlight cells E2 to E4

21. Click 🔳 to return to the Edit Series dialog box

Figure 102

22. Press 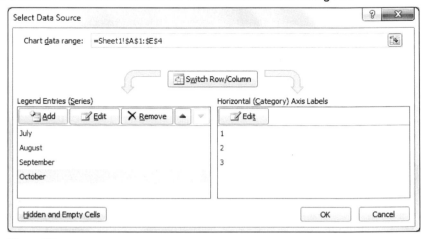 OK to return to the Select Data Source dialog box

Figure 103

23. Press OK to return to the updated chart

Changing the Type of Chart

1. Click in the chart, select Design , choose Change Chart Type

2. Select the chart type 100% Stacked Horizontal Cylinder

3. Press OK

4. To change the style of chart, select Design

5. Choose Chart Style 15

6. The chart is updated automatically

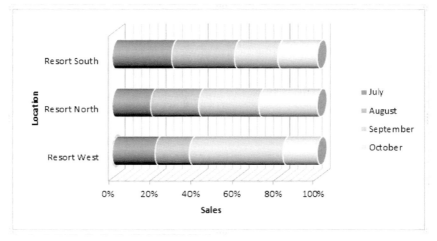

Figure 104

7. To remove the minor gridlines, click anywhere on the chart

8. Move the mouse pointer ⌕ over one of the minor gridlines

9. The following prompt appears Horizontal (Value) Axis Major Gridlines

10. Click with the left 🖰 button to select the minor gridlines

11. Press Delete

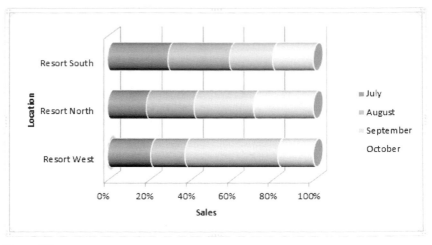

Figure 105

12. To change the background colour of the chart

13. Move the mouse pointer ⬉ on the back wall of the chart, [Back Wall] appears

14. Click with the left 🖱 button, blue circles ○ appear around the selected area

15. Click with the right 🖱 button, select ☞ Format Back Wall...

16. Select ◉ Gradient fill

17. Choose the background colour using the downward arrow

18. Press [Close]

19. To change the colour of the floor

20. Move the mouse pointer ⬉ onto the floor area, [Floor] appears on the chart

21. Click with the right 🖱 button, select ☞ Format Floor...

22. Select ◉ Solid fill, choose the background colour Color: [🎨 ▾]

23. Select [Close]

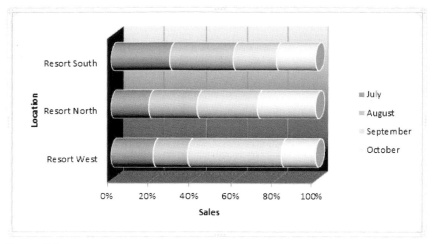

Figure 106

Adding Data Labels

1. Move the mouse pointer ⟲ over the October Series in the chart

2. Click with the right ⊖ button, select   Add Data Labels

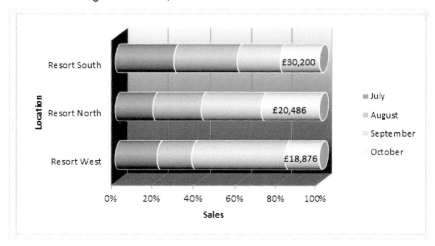

Figure 107

3. To format the data labels

4. Click with the right ⊖ button over the area, select 📄 Format Data Labels...

5. The Format Data Labels dialog box appears

Figure 108

6. Select 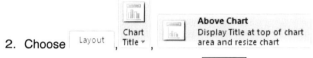 ✓ Series Name from the Label Options area

7. Deselect ☐ Value, press [Close]

8. October appears as the Data Label [October]

Adding a Title to the Chart

1. Select the chart to display the Chart Tools

2. Choose [Layout], [Chart Title ▾], **Above Chart** Display Title at top of chart area and resize chart

3. Type Customising Charts, press [Enter]

Changing a Chart using 3-D Rotation

1. Move the mouse pointer ⌖ over the back wall of the chart

2. Press the right 🖱 button on the wall of the chart

3. Select 🗋 3-D Rotation... , the Format Chart Area dialog box appears

Figure 109

4. Change the Rotation as required

5. Ensure Right Angle A**x**es is **not** selected

6. Click Close to return to the chart

Changing the Style of Chart

1. Select Design , Change Chart Type

2. The Change Chart Type dialog box appears

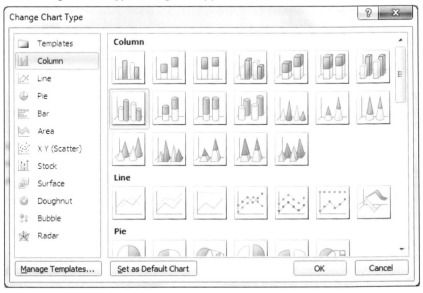

Figure 110

3. Select the chart type required, press OK

Figure 111

Interpreting Data in Charts

Charts can show the same data but in different formats allowing data to be interpreted in different ways.

1. Open the workbook Working with Charts

2. Click with the right  button inside the chart area

3. Choose Change Chart Type , select [Line] , [Stacked line with Markers]

4. Press [OK]

Saving a Chart as a Template

1. Click inside the chart area, the [Chart Tools Design Layout Format] Tab appears

2. Choose [Design] , Save As Template , the Save Chart Template dialog box appears

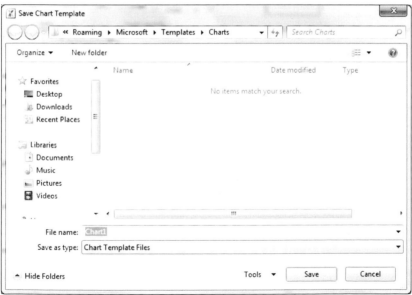

Figure 112

3. Create a name for the Chart Template and a description

4. Press [Save]

Vertical and Horizontal Lookup Functions

Lookup functions are useful to locate data in a selected table, database or list. Vertical Lookup (VLOOKUP) searches for a value in the left most column of a table and then returns a value in the same row from the selected column in the table, database or list. Horizontal Lookup (HLOOKUP) searches for a value in the top row of the table, database or list and returns a value in the same column from the selected row.

Vertical Lookup

1. Select a new worksheet, generate the following information

	A	B	C	D	E
1			Sales		
2	**Name**	**2005**	**2006**	**2007**	**2008**
3	Debbie Jones	£25,000	£25,950	£28,375	£27,760
4	Robert Flinn	£25,465	£26,790	£27,750	£27,060
5	Jane Haworth	£28,945	£26,345	£28,900	£26,100
6	Donald Stewart	£24,670	£25,350	£22,575	£26,395
7	Jason Burton	£27,500	£25,435	£23,799	£21,356
8	Elizabeth Roberts	£25,675	£25,300	£26,987	£28,103
9	Leslie Harvey	£21,945	£28,545	£23,765	£22,100
10	Denise Willington	£26,970	£27,600	£27,150	£27,390
11	Andrew Gerrard	£24,545	£23,900	£23,750	£24,100

Figure 113

2. Create the tabled information below to use in the vlookup formula

	A	B
22	**Commission Payments**	
23	£25,000	1.00%
24	£25,500	1.50%
25	£26,000	2.00%
26	£26,500	2.50%
27	£27,000	3.00%
28	£27,500	3.50%
29	£28,000	4.00%
30	£28,500	4.50%

Figure 114

3. Highlight cells A23:B30

4. Select Formulas

5. Choose Define Name from the Defined Names Grouping

6. The New Name dialog box appears

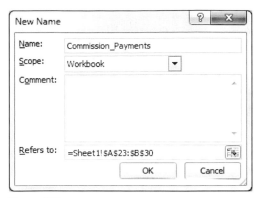

Figure 115

7. Type Commission_Payments in the **N**ame box

8. Click [OK]

9. Create the following information in cells A16 and A18

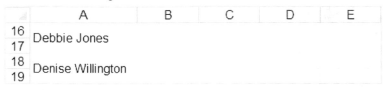

Figure 116

10. To create a vlookup formula for quarterly commission payments as a %

11. Click in cell B16

12. Type **=vlookup(B3,Commission_Payments,2)**, press [Enter]

Note: B3 in the formula represents Debbie Jones's Sales volume for the year 2005, Commission_Payments represents the named area used in the formula and the number 2 instructs the formula to look at the information in column 2.

13. The result is 1% in cell B16

14. Click in cell B16, use the black fill handle to drag to E16

15. Format the cells into a percentage format

16. To calculate the formula as a £ value

17. Select cell B17 type =B3*B16 to calculate the amount of commission

18. This represents £25,000 multiplied by 1%

19. Drag the relative formula to cell E17

20. Follow the steps to complete the information for Denise Willington

21. The results are outlined below

	A	B	C	D	E
16	Debbie Jones	1.00%	1.50%	4.00%	3.50%
17		£250.00	£389.25	£1,135.00	£971.60
18	Denise Willington	2.50%	3.50%	3.00%	3.00%
19		£674.25	£966.00	£814.50	£821.70

Figure 117

Horizontal Lookup

The formula for horizontal lookup is, select the column, select the table, select the row.

	A	B	C	D	E	F	G	H
1	**Name**	**January**	**February**	**March**	**April**	**May**	**June**	**Totals**
2	Goods In	£5,890.00	£4,671.00	£5,891.00	£4,998.00	£3,297.00	£3,789.00	£28,536.00
3	Sewing	£7,902.00	£7,857.00	£7,985.00	£6,342.00	£6,876.00	£7,203.00	£44,165.00
4	Tooling	£9,230.00	£7,350.00	£6,892.00	£5,890.00	£6,003.00	£5,907.00	£41,272.00
5	Spraying	£9,890.00	£7,750.00	£5,999.00	£6,002.00	£7,090.00	£6,325.00	£43,056.00
6	Maintenance	£11,009.00	£12,340.00	£15,700.00	£11,786.00	£10,906.00	£10,870.00	£72,611.00
7	Despatch	£14,560.00	£16,900.00	£15,650.00	£14,340.00	£14,980.00	£16,987.00	£93,417.00
8	Material	£15,900.00	£16,723.00	£17,230.00	£16,800.00	£15,236.00	£14,009.00	£95,898.00
9	Export	£17,340.00	£17,551.00	£17,340.00	£16,996.00	£18,000.00	£17,909.00	£105,136.00
10	**Totals**	£91,721.00	£91,142.00	£92,687.00	£83,154.00	£82,388.00	£82,999.00	

Figure 118

1. Open a new workbook, create the above table

2. Format the cells as shown

3. Highlight cells A1 to H10, select Formulas

4. Choose Define Name from the Defined Names Grouping

5. The New Name dialog box appears

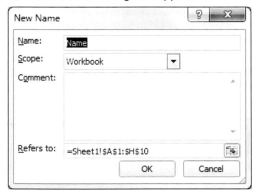

Figure 119

6. Type Production in the **N**ame box, click OK

7. Using hlookup create a table that displays

    a. The monthly costs for Goods In for the months of January and May

    b. The results for January and May Goods In are £5,890 and £3,297

	A	B	C
28		**January**	**May**
29	Goods In	=hlookup(B1,Production,2)	=hlookup(F1,Production,2)

Figure 120

8. Save the workbook as Using Horizontal Lookup

Note: Unlike vlookup, hlookup formulas are created individually. Displayed above is the result for January Goods In & May Goods In, the word "Production" relates to the defined area A1:H10.

Exercise 7: - Using Horizontal Lookup

1. Open the workbook Using Horizontal Lookup
2. Using hlookup update the table to include
    a. The monthly costs for Despatch and Export for the months of January and May
    b. The Total costs for Goods In, Despatch and Export

	A	B	C	D
28		**January**	**May**	**Totals**
29	Goods In	£5,890.00	£3,297.00	
30	Despatch			
31	Export			

3. Save the workbook

Working with Comments

Excel allows you to insert comments to a cell that can easily be viewed or printed.

Inserting Comments

1. Open an existing workbook, click in a cell

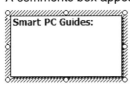

2. Select Review , choose New Comment

3. A comments box appears

Figure 121

4. Alternatively press SHIFT   F2   to display the comments box

5. Type the required text

6. Click outside the comment to deselect

7. A red ◥ marker appears in the cell containing the comment

Viewing Comments

1. Move the cursor into the cell containing the comment

2. The comments box appears

3. To deselect, move the cursor outside the cell

4. Alternatively press F5 , the Go To dialog box appears

Figure 122

5. Select [Special...]

6. The Go To Special dialog box appears

Figure 123

7. Select Comments, click [OK]

8. All the cells containing comments are highlighted

9. To view any comment move the mouse pointer ⌖ over the highlighted cell

Editing Comments

Edit
Comment

1. Select [Review], click in the cell that contains a comment, choose

2. Amend the comment, click back in the cell with the edited comment

3. The edited comment is displayed

Deleting Comments

Delete

1. Select [Review], choose

2. The comment is deleted from the cell

Show all Comments in a Worksheet

1. To display all the comments, choose [Show All Comments]

2. To hide all the comments, reselect [Show All Comments]

Show/Hide Comments in Selected Cells

1. Click on a cell that contains a comment

2. Choose [Show/Hide Comment] , the comment is displayed

3. To hide the comment, reselect [Show/Hide Comment]

Moving a Comments Box

1. Click on [Show All Comments]

2. Position the cursor over the edge of the comments box

3. Click with the left 🖱 button, drag to the new location

Adjusting the Size of a Comments Box

1. Select [Show All Comments]

2. Position the cursor over the edge of the comments box

3. Press the left 🖱 button, using the resizing handles drag to the new size

Printing Comments

1. Select Page Layout , choose the Page Setup Grouping

2. Click with the left 🖱 button on the dialog box launcher ⬚

3. The Page Setup dialog box appears

4. Select the Sheet Tab

Figure 124

5. In the Comments area, select As displayed on sheet or At end of sheet

6. Press Print Preview to display the comments on the worksheet

7. Choose ▸ to display the comments throughout the worksheet

8. Press  or ESC to return to the worksheet

Password Protection

Excel provides several ways to restrict access to a workbook or prevent changes to the structure of a workbook, such as moving, deleting or adding sheets by assigning a password.

IMPORTANT INFORMATION ABOUT YOUR PASWORD – WRITE IT DOWN AND KEEP IT SAFE. **If you lose the password, you cannot open or gain access to the data in the password protected workbook.**

Protecting the Structure of a Workbook

1. Open a workbook

2. Click on   Review , select Protect Workbook from the Changes Grouping

3. The Protect Structure and Windows dialog box appears

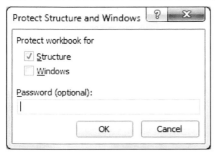

Figure 125

4. Place a tick ☑ in the **S**tructure box to protect the structure of the workbook

5. Passwords are case sensitive

6. In the **P**assword (optional) box type in a password of your choice

7. Press ⌊___OK___⌋

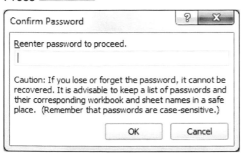

Figure 126

8. Re-enter the password, click [OK], save the workbook

9. To alter the structure of the workbook, for example adding a new worksheet

10. Double click with the left button on sheet 1

11. The following dialog box appears

Figure 127

12. Click [OK]

13. Press the right button over any of the sheet tabs

14. The structure of the workbook is protected

15. The user cannot insert, delete or move sheets

16. Alternatively select on [File], [Info]

17. The permissions area highlights the workbook has been locked

Permissions

The structure of the workbook has been locked to prevent unwanted changes, such as moving, deleting, or adding sheets.

Protect
Workbook ⁻

Figure 128

Protection Options using the File Tab

1. Click with the left 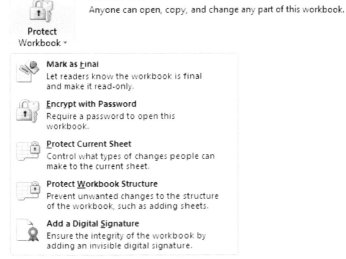 button on [File], [Info]

2. In the Permissions area select Protect Workbook

3. The following dialog options appear

Protect Workbook ▾

Permissions
Anyone can open, copy, and change any part of this workbook.

Mark as Final
Let readers know the workbook is final and make it read-only.

Encrypt with Password
Require a password to open this workbook.

Protect Current Sheet
Control what types of changes people can make to the current sheet.

Protect Workbook Structure
Prevent unwanted changes to the structure of the workbook, such as adding sheets.

Add a Digital Signature
Ensure the integrity of the workbook by adding an invisible digital signature.

Figure 129

4. Select the required option

Changing a Password

1. Open a workbook

2. Select **File** , 🖫 Save As

3. Click Tools ▼ from the bottom of the Save As dialog box

4. Choose   General Options...

5. The General Options dialog box appears

Figure 130

6. Select Password to **m**odify, type in the new password

7. Click   OK

8. The Confirm Password dialog box appears

9. Retype the password

Figure 131

10. Press   OK   , save the workbook

Removing a Password

1. Open a workbook, click Review

2. Select Workbook from the Changes Grouping

3. The Unprotect Workbook dialog appears

Figure 132

4. Type in the password to be deleted, press OK

5. Save the workbook

Protecting a Sheet

1. Open a workbook, click Review

2. Select Sheet from the Changes Grouping

3. The Protect Sheet dialog box appears

Figure 133

4. Click OK

5. Alternatively type a password, **R**e-enter password again, press OK

Protecting a Range

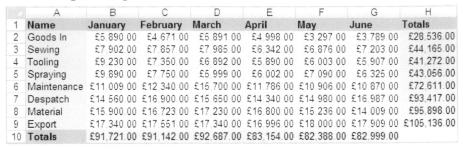

	A	B	C	D	E	F	G	H
1	Name	January	February	March	April	May	June	Totals
2	Goods In	£5,890.00	£4,671.00	£5,891.00	£4,998.00	£3,297.00	£3,789.00	£28,536.00
3	Sewing	£7,902.00	£7,857.00	£7,985.00	£6,342.00	£6,876.00	£7,203.00	£44,165.00
4	Tooling	£9,230.00	£7,350.00	£6,892.00	£5,890.00	£6,003.00	£5,907.00	£41,272.00
5	Spraying	£9,890.00	£7,750.00	£5,999.00	£6,002.00	£7,090.00	£6,325.00	£43,056.00
6	Maintenance	£11,009.00	£12,340.00	£15,700.00	£11,786.00	£10,906.00	£10,870.00	£72,611.00
7	Despatch	£14,560.00	£16,900.00	£15,650.00	£14,340.00	£14,980.00	£16,987.00	£93,417.00
8	Material	£15,900.00	£16,723.00	£17,230.00	£16,800.00	£15,236.00	£14,009.00	£95,898.00
9	Export	£17,340.00	£17,551.00	£17,340.00	£16,996.00	£18,000.00	£17,909.00	£105,136.00
10	Totals	£91,721.00	£91,142.00	£92,687.00	£83,154.00	£82,388.00	£82,999.00	

Figure 134

1. Open the workbook Using Horizontal Lookup
2. Click Review, select Allow Users to Edit Ranges from the Change Grouping
3. The Allow Users to Edit Ranges dialog box appears

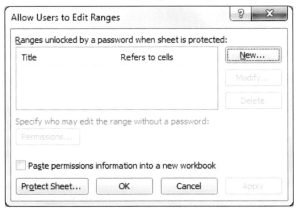

Figure 135

4. Select New..., the New Range dialog box appears

Figure 136

5. Type January in the Title area

6. Select 🔳 in the Refers to cells area

7. Select cells B2:B10, click 🔳 to confirm the range

8. In the Range password area, type January

9. Click [OK], re-enter the password, press [OK]

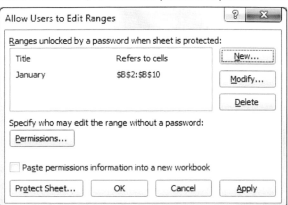

Title

January $B$2:$B$10

Specify who may edit the range without a password:

Permissions...

☐ Paste permissions information into a new workbook

Protect Sheet...   OK   Cancel   Apply

Figure 137

10. Select [Protect Sheet...]

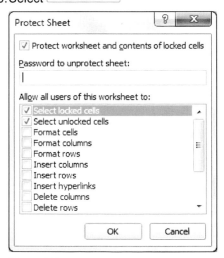

Figure 138

11. Select [OK] and save the worksheet

12. Click in cell F5, try to change the data in this cell

13. The following prompt appears

Figure 139

14. Alternatively double click in cell B8, the following dialog box appears

Figure 140

15. Enter January in the password area, click OK

16. Amendments to the selected range can now be made

17. Save and close the workbook

Filtering Data

Sorting and filtering large amounts of data within a worksheet using the AutoFilter and Advanced Filter is a useful way of displaying data as a sub-section view.

Sorting and Filtering Data

	A	B	C	D	E	F	G	H
1	Location	Section	Surname	First Name	DOB	Start Date	Job Title	Salary
2	Birmingham	Sales	Stuart	Bernard	16/01/1972	01/10/1991	Clerk	£9,878
3	Canterbury	Marketing	James	Brenda	27/11/1980	19/08/2001	Manager	£32,156
4	Cardiff	Buying	Russell	David	16/06/1963	10/11/2000	Buyer	£25,075
5	Cheltenham	Buying	Naylor	John	08/04/1981	03/06/2003	Buyer	£25,075
6	Edinburgh	Logistics	Bridges	Victoria	08/01/1957	08/08/1989	Manager	£20,650
7	Glasgow	Training	Andrews	Nicola	13/10/1967	15/07/1990	Training Officer	£27,456
8	Glasgow	Research	Williams	Charles	26/03/1972	01/01/1992	Manager	£30,276
9	Glasgow	Payroll	Middleton	Richard	08/02/1958	02/01/1988	Payroll Clerk	£9,878
10	Manchester	IT	Charles	Rose	21/10/1970	07/12/2000	Technician	£28,743
11	Newcastle	Accounts	Bagstaff	Samuel	14/07/1963	12/12/1985	Accountant	£28,300
12	Norwich	IT	Phillips	Mark	05/05/1976	29/09/1996	Technician	£27,090
13	Norwich	Sales	Osborne	Sara	16/05/1965	17/07/1984	Tele Sales	£16,970
14	Reading	HR	Kane	Lauren	09/03/1954	27/03/1976	HR Officer	£33,276

Figure 141

1. Open a blank new workbook, create the above data within a worksheet

2. Save the workbook as Sorting and Filtering Data

3. Click in cell A6, select   Data

4. Choose Sort ↓ from the Sort and Filter Grouping

5. The worksheet is updated automatically sorted by Location in Alphabetical order

Filtering Data using Several Criteria

To generate a sort using the criteria section in ascending order, Job Title in ascending order and Salary in descending order.

1. Select a cell that contains the data to be sorted, choose Data

2. Click with the the left button on Sort from Sort and Filter Grouping

3. The Sort dialog box appears

Figure 142

4. In the Sort by box, select Section and Order A to Z, select Add Level

5. In the Then by box, select Job Title and Order A to Z, select Add Level

6. In the Then by box select, Salary and Order Smallest to Largest

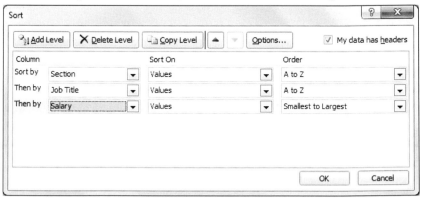

Figure 143

7. Click OK

Filter Icon

Filter

1. Click on a cell containing the list of data, select `Data` , choose

2. A downward arrow `▾` is displayed in each relevant column heading

3. Click on the arrow in the heading Section `▾`

4. Select Buying, IT and Marketing, click `OK`

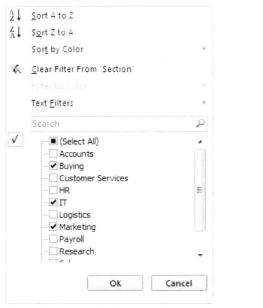

Figure 144

5. The filter icon `⊤` appears when a filter is applied in the Column Heading

6. Members of staff in the Buying, IT and Marketing sections are displayed

	A	B	C	D	E	F	G	H
1	Location ▾	Section ⊤	Surname ▾	First Name ▾	DOB ▾	Start Date ▾	Job Title ▾	Salary ▾
3	Canterbury	Marketing	James	Brenda	27/11/1980	19/08/2001	Manager	£32,156
4	Cardiff	Buying	Russell	David	16/06/1963	10/11/2000	Buyer	£25,075
5	Cheltenham	Buying	Naylor	John	08/04/1981	03/06/2003	Buyer	£25,075
10	Manchester	IT	Charles	Rose	21/10/1970	07/12/2000	Technician	£28,743
12	Norwich	IT	Phillips	Mark	05/05/1976	29/09/1996	Technician	£27,090

Figure 145

7. Row numbers that match the criteria change to blue

8. To remove the filter click on the filter icon `⊤`

9. Choose `✖ Clear Filter From "Section"` , or `☑ (Select All)`

10. press `OK`

Creating a Custom Filter

1. Click on the arrow in the heading **Salary** ▾

2. Select Number Filters ▸ , Equals...

3. The Custom AutoFilter dialog box appears

4. Complete the Custom AutoFilter as shown

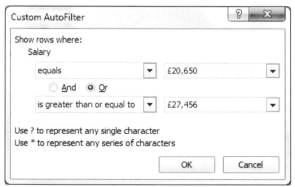

Figure 146

5. Click [OK], the data is displayed as follows

	A	B	C	D	E	F	G	H
1	Location ▾	Section ▾	Surname ▾	First Name ▾	DOB ▾	Start Date ▾	Job Title ▾	Salary ▾
3	Canterbury	Marketing	James	Brenda	27/11/1980	19/08/2001	Manager	£32,156
6	Edinburgh	Logistics	Bridges	Victoria	08/01/1957	08/08/1989	Manager	£20,650
7	Glasgow	Training	Andrews	Nicola	13/10/1967	15/07/1990	Training Office	£27,456
8	Glasgow	Research	Williams	Charles	26/03/1972	01/01/1992	Manager	£30,276
10	Manchester	IT	Charles	Rose	21/10/1970	07/12/2000	Technician	£28,743
11	Newcastle	Accounts	Bagstaff	Samuel	14/07/1963	12/12/1985	Accountant	£28,300
14	Reading	HR	Kane	Lauren	09/03/1954	27/03/1976	HR Officer	£33,276

Figure 147

6. Create a custom filter of your choice based upon the salary data

Advanced Filter

The Advanced Filter is used to create more complex criteria to be filtered.

1. Using the workbook Sorting and Filtering Data

2. Click in a blank cell beneath the main data

3. Type or copy the headings for the advanced filter as shown below

Location	Salary	Salary
Norwich	>=17250	
Glasgow	>=18000	<=34000

Figure 148

4. In this instance the advanced filter has been asked to locate staff with salaries greater than or equal to £17,250 in Norwich and salaries greater than or equal to £18,000 but less than or equal to £34,000 in Glasgow

5. Click anywhere in the original data

6. Sort the location field into alphabetical order

7. Select Data , choose Advanced from the Sort & Filter Grouping

8. The Advanced Filter dialog box appears

Figure 149

9. A dotted line appears around the original data

10. In this example, click with the left button to Copy to another location

11. Press TAB , the original data is highlighted in the List range area

12. Select TAB to move to the Criteria range

13. Click the icon to select the advanced criteria including the headings

14. Click the icon to return to the Advanced Filter dialog box

15. Press TAB to move to Copy to

16. Click in cell A30, choose OK

17. The results are shown below

	A	B	C	D	E	F	G	H
30	**Location**	**Section**	**Surname**	**First Name**	**DOB**	**Start Date**	**Job Title**	**Salary**
31	Glasgow	Training	Andrews	Nicola	13/10/1967	15/07/1990	Training Officer	£27,456
32	Glasgow	Research	Williams	Charles	26/03/1972	01/01/1992	Manager	£30,276
33	Norwich	IT	Phillips	Mark	05/05/1976	29/09/1996	Technician	£27,090

Figure 150

Exercise 8: - Using the Advanced Filter

1. Open the workbook Sorting and Filtering Data
2. Set the criteria to find staff based in Birmingham, Manchester and Norwich
3. Copy the advanced filter to another location
4. The result shows four people that match the criteria
5. Return to the original data
6. Using the advanced filter, define the criteria to find Mark Phillips and Rose Charles
7. The results show the data on Mark Philips and Rose Charles
8. Return to the original data
9. Save the workbook

Subtotals Feature

1. Open the workbook Sorting and Filtering Data

2. Click anywhere in the original data

3. Sort the Section area into alphabetical order

Subtotal

4. Select Data , choose   from the Outline Grouping

5. The Subtotal dialog box appears

6. Select the following criteria

Figure 151

7. Click [OK   ], the results are shown below

1 2 3		A	B	C	D	E	F	G	H
	1	**Location**	**Section**	**Surname**	**First Name**	**DOB**	**Start Date**	**Job Title**	**Salary**
	2	Newcastle	Accounts	Bagstaff	Samuel	14/07/1963	12/12/1985	Accountant	£28,300
	3		**Accounts Total**						£28,300
	4	Cardiff	Buying	Russell	David	16/06/1963	10/11/2000	Buyer	£25,075
	5	Cheltenham	Buying	Naylor	John	08/04/1981	03/06/2003	Buyer	£25,075
	6		**Buying Total**						£50,150

Figure 152

8. There are 3 outline icons to the left of Column A [1][2][3]

9. Select 1 to display the grand total

10. Select 2 to display the section totals

11. Select 3 to display all the criteria

Removing Subtotals

1. Click in the original data

2. Select Data , choose **Subtotal** from the Outline Grouping

3. Select Remove All

Section 3

Expert Level Objectives

Range Names

When working in Excel a cell or block of cells can be defined using meaningful names, for example =sum(A2:D2) can be defined as =Sum(Leeds:Leicester). Names can also be applied to formulas.

Advantages of Range Names

1. It is easier to remember a name rather than a cell reference

2. Formulas are easier to understand

3. When a name is redefined all formulas using the name are updated

4. Using Range Names makes navigation around a worksheet faster

Define a Range Name

1. Click with the left 🖱 button in a cell or selected range of cells

2. Select ‌Formulas‌ , choose ‌Define Name ▾‌

3. The New Name dialog box appears

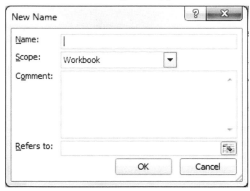

Figure 153

4. In the **N**ame box, define a specific name for the range of cells

5. In the **S**cope box select workbook or the sheet the range name refers to

6. In the C**o**mment box enter a descriptive comment

7. The **R**efers to box highlights the selected cell or range of cells

8. Click ‌OK‌

9. Click in any cell outside the selected range

10. Move the cursor to the Name Box area ‌...‌ on the Formula Bar

11. Click on the downward pointing arrow ▾, select the newly defined name

12. The range is highlighted

Delete a Defined Name

1. Select Formulas , choose Name Manager or press CTRL F3

2. The Name Manager dialog box appears

3. Click with the left 🖰 button on the name to be deleted, press Delete

4. Select OK

5. Choose Close

Create a Range of Names

Using the 'create from selection' feature allows multiple names to be created in one instruction.

1. Create the following information

	A	B	C	D
1	**Newspaper Sales**	**January**	**February**	**March**
2	The Daily Telegraph	12090	13009	13090
3	The Mail	15102	15602	15765
4	The Guardian	11090	10358	10975
5	Financial Times	8759	9035	8950
6	Total	47041	48004	48780

Figure 154

2. Highlight cells A1:D5

3. Select Formulas , choose, 🖼 Create from Selection

4. The Create Names from Selection dialog box appears

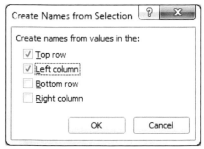

Figure 155

5. Select **T**op row and **L**eft Column, click OK

6. Move the cursor to the Name Box area on the Formula Bar

7. Click the downward pointing arrow ▾, select "The Mail", the data is highlighted

Apply Names Feature

Using formulas in the selected area before names are applied means formula names are not displayed, in order for the formula to be displayed, a name has to be applied.

	A	B	C	D
1	**Newspaper Sales**	**January**	**February**	**March**
2	The Daily Telegraph	12090	13009	13090
3	The Mail	15102	15602	15765
4	The Guardian	11090	10358	10975
5	Financial Times	8759	9035	8950
6	Total	47041	48004	48780

Figure 156

1. Highlight cells A1:D6

2. Select   Formulas   , click on the downward arrow on   Define Name

3. Choose   Apply Names...   , the Apply Names dialog box appears

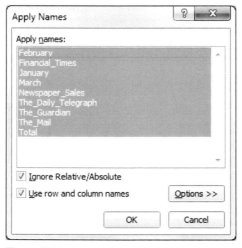

Figure 157

4. Choose   OK   , the names have been applied

5. Click in cell B6, C6 and D6, the names have been applied to the formulas

6. Select an empty cell, type =The_Mail January + The_Guardian January

7. Press   Enter   , the total for The Mail and The Guardian for January is displayed

8. Select cell E2, type =SUM(The_Daily_Telegraph)

9. Press   Enter   , the total for The Daily Telegraph is displayed

10. Select cell E3, type =The_Mail January + February + March

11. Press 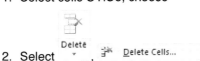, the total for The Mail for January, February and March is displayed

12. Create the totals for The Guardian and the Financial Times

Delete a Range of Names

1. Select cells C1:C6, choose Home

2. Select Delete ▾ , ⊒✳ Delete Cells...

3. The Delete dialog box appears, select ⊙ Entire column

4. Select OK

Delete	?	X
Delete		
○ Shift cells left		
○ Shift cells up		
○ Entire row		
⊙ Entire column		
OK	Cancel	

Figure 158

5. If a total displays #REF! when data has been deleted, the total will need to be recalculated by deleting February from the formula

6. Save the workbook as Working with Names and Ranges

Display Range Names

To view an index of the range names applied in a worksheet.

1. Click in the empty cell H1 to display the information

2. Select [Formulas] , choose fx Use in Formula ▾ ,   Paste Names... ,

3. The Paste Name dialog box appears

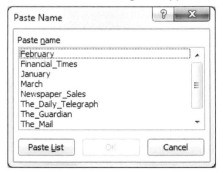

Figure 159

4. Select [Paste List] , the applied names and references are displayed

February	=Sheet1!$C$2:$C$6
Financial_Times	=Sheet1!$B$5:$D$5
January	=Sheet1!$B$2:$B$6
March	=Sheet1!$D$2:$D$6
Newspaper_Sales	=Sheet1!$B$2:$D$6
The_Daily_Telegraph	=Sheet1!$B$2:$D$2
The_Guardian	=Sheet1!$B$4:$D$4
The_Mail	=Sheet1!$B$3:$D$3

Figure 160

Note: **The list will not automatically update if new names are added.**

Auditing Functions

Excel allows formulas and results in a worksheet to be traced using the Formula Auditing Grouping.

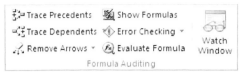

Figure 161

Trace Precedent/Dependent Features

1. Create the following worksheet

	A	B	C	D	E	F	G
1	**Sales**	**January**	**February**	**March**	**April**	**May**	**Total**
2							
3	**Monday**	11500	14000	11125	11765	15122	63512
4	**Tuesday**	12000	14001	13234	11000	13245	63480
5	**Wednesday**	14000	14002	12678	11200	19174	71054
6	**Thursday**	16000	14003	10976	11300	13328	65607
7	**Friday**	18000	14004	16740	11400	19884	80028
8	**Saturday**	20000	14005	10308	11500	19487	75300
9	**Sunday**	22000	14006	13444	11600	16029	77079
10							
11	**Monthly Total**	113500	98021	88505	79765	116269	

Figure 162

2. Select cell G3, choose **Formulas**, click on the **Trace Precedents** icon
3. Tracer arrows display the cells that provide data to the formula

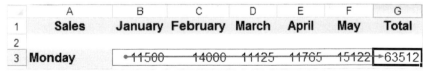

Figure 163

4. To remove the arrows click on the **Remove Arrows** icon
5. Select cell C6, click on **Trace Dependents**

	A	B	C	D	E	F	G
1	**Sales**	**January**	**February**	**March**	**April**	**May**	**Total**
2							
3	**Monday**	11500	14000	11125	11765	15122	63512
4	**Tuesday**	12000	14001	13234	11000	13245	63480
5	**Wednesday**	14000	14002	12678	11200	19174	71054
6	**Thursday**	16000	14003	10976	11300	13328	65607
7	**Friday**	18000	14004	16740	11400	19884	80028
8	**Saturday**	20000	14005	10308	11500	19487	75300
9	**Sunday**	22000	14006	13444	11600	16029	77079
10							
11	**Monthly Total**	113500	98021	88505	79765	116269	

Figure 164

6. Tracer arrows highlight the cells containing data to the formula

7. To remove the arrows click on   Remove Arrows

8. Save the Workbook as Using Auditing Functions

Trace Error Features

1. If an error occurs, select the cell containing the error message

2. Choose   Error Checking

3. The Error Checking dialog box appears, displaying the cell reference

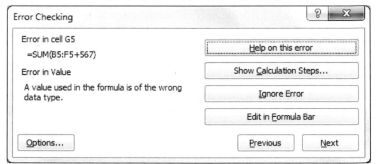

Figure 165

4. Choose   Next   to identify the type of error

5. Press   Edit in Formula Bar

6. Amend the reference manually

7. Select the ✓ to accept the change, choose   Resume

Figure 166

8. Click

Note: **The Trace Error Feature will display errors in any worksheet within an open workbook. If formulas are contained in another workbook that workbook needs to be opened to complete the full check.**

Watch Window Feature

The Watch Window feature allows the user to monitor the values of cells.

1. Open the workbook named Using Auditing Functions

2. Rename the worksheet as Monthly Sales Figures

3. Select Watch Window from the Formula Auditing Grouping

4. The Watch Window dialog box appears

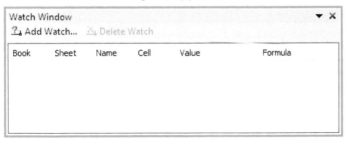

Figure 167

5. Highlight cells G3:G9, choose ?☐ Add Watch... , the Add Watch window appears

Figure 168

6. Click Add , the highlighted cells appear in the Watch Window

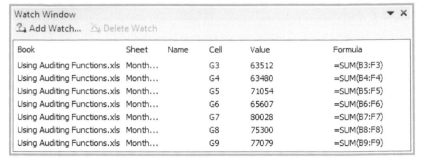

Figure 169

7. Select cell B11, add the Monthly Total to the Watch Window

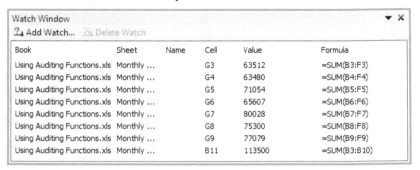

Figure 170

8. Add cells C11,D11,E11 and F11 to the Watch Window

9. To delete a Watch Window reference, select the item, press ⟨Delete Watch⟩

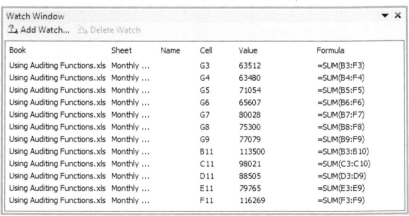

Figure 171

Items within the Watch Window

1. The Watch Window displays the name of the Workbook, Sheet, Cell, Value and Formula
2. The user can watch cells and their formulas even when out of view
3. To display formulas in another workbook, the workbook must be opened
4. A defined name for a formula is displayed in the Name area
5. To sort by value, select Value

Conditional Formatting

Conditional formatting allows the user to quickly identify variances in a range of values by applying a colour scale to differentiate high, medium, and low values. To apply conditional formatting

10. Select the data where conditionally formatting is required
11. Alternatively type the following table

	A	B	C	D	E	F	G	H
1				% Sales				
2		January	Ferbuary	March	April	May	June	6 Monthly Performance
3	Book	33	27	26	22	24	28	
4	Newspaper	78	74	77	73	72	71	
5	Magazine	55	56	47	57	47	57	

Figure 172

12. Select the cells B3:G5 or the cells requiring formatting

13. Choose Home , Conditional Formatting , Data Bars

14. Choose Gradient Fill Orange , the formatting is applied to the table

	A	B	C	D	E	F	G	H
1				% Sales				
2		January	Ferbuary	March	April	May	June	6 Monthly Performance
3	Book	33	27	26	22	24	28	
4	Newspaper	78	74	77	73	72	71	
5	Magazine	55	56	47	57	47	57	

Figure 173

15. Re-select the cells to apply additional formatting

16. Choose 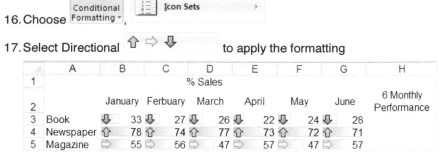,

17. Select Directional ⇧ ⇨ ⇩ to apply the formatting

	A	B	C	D	E	F	G	H
1				% Sales				
2		January	Ferbuary	March	April	May	June	6 Monthly Performance
3	Book	⇩ 33 ⇩	27 ⇩	26 ⇩	22 ⇩	24 ⇩	28	
4	Newspaper	⇧ 78 ⇧	74 ⇧	77 ⇧	73 ⇧	72 ⇧	71	
5	Magazine	⇨ 55 ⇨	56 ⇨	47 ⇨	57 ⇨	47 ⇨	57	

Figure 174

18. Save the workbook as Conditional Formatting

Sparkline Formatting

A sparkline is a tiny chart in a worksheet cell that provides a visual representation of the data in the worksheet. Although data presented in a row or column is useful, patterns can be hard to spot at a glance. Sparklines take up a small amount of room and display a trend based on adjacent data in a clear and compact graphical representation allowing a quick relationship between a sparkline and its underlying data to be seen. When data changes in the worksheet the change can be seen immediately in the sparkline. To apply sparkline formatting

1. Open the workbook Conditional Formatting

	A	B	C	D	E	F	G	H
1				% Sales				
2		January	Ferbuary	March	April	May	June	6 Monthly Performance
3	Book	⇩ 33 ⇩	27 ⇩	26 ⇩	22 ⇩	24 ⇩	28	
4	Newspaper	⇧ 78 ⇧	74 ⇧	77 ⇧	73 ⇧	72 ⇧	71	
5	Magazine	⇨ 55 ⇨	56 ⇨	47 ⇨	57 ⇨	47 ⇨	57	

Figure 175

2. Alternatively select the worksheet where a sparkline is to appear

3. Select cell H3, choose 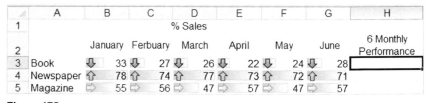, from the Sparklines Grouping

4. The Create Sparklines dialog box appears

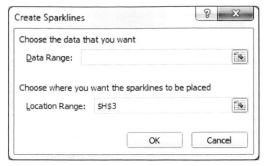

Figure 176

5. Click on the Data Range  icon

6. Select cells B3:G3, click on the Data Range icon to return to the Create Sparklines dialog box

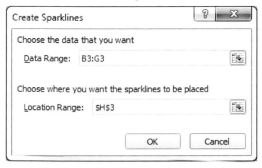

Figure 177

7. Click on the Location Range icon

8. Select cell H3, click back on the Location Range icon

9. Select [OK], the sparkline appears in the worksheet

10. Repeat the above process to create Sparklines for cells H4 and H5

11. Alternatively select cell H3, use the black fill handle to copy the sparkline format to cells H4 and H5

12. Click in cell H3, the [Sparkline Tools] Tab appears, select [Design]

13. Select Markers ☑ Markers from the Show Grouping

14. Markers appear in the sparkline

15. Choose [Design] , ■ Marker Color ▾ , ◪ Markers ▸

16. Select the colour Red, or the colour required

17. The sparkline displays markers showing the trend representing each month

	A	B	C	D	E	F	G	H
1				% Sales				
2		January	Ferbuary	March	April	May	June	6 Monthly Performance
3	Book	⬇ 33	⬇ 27	⬇ 26	⬇ 22	⬇ 24	⬇ 28	
4	Newspaper	⬆ 78	⬆ 74	⬆ 77	⬆ 73	⬆ 72	71	
5	Magazine	➡ 55	➡ 56	➡ 47	➡ 57	➡ 47	57	

Figure 178

18. Save and close the workbook

Strings and Text Functions

A string is a sequence of characters entered as a label in Excel. Labels used in formulas are String Values. Formulas that contain more than one string value are referred to as string expressions and must begin with an = (equal symbol). String expressions joined together are concatenated. The following example displays how concatenation works.

	A	B	C	D	E
1	**First Name**	**Surname**	**Result**	**Formula**	**Explanation**
2	Robert	Smith	Robert Smith	=A2&" "&B2	Join cells A2 & B2 with a space between cells
3	Peter	Richards	PETER RICHARDS	=UPPER(A3&" "&B3)	Upper case, join cells A3 & B3, space between cells
4	Tony	Parker	tony parker	=LOWER(A4&" "&B4)	Lower case, join cells A4 & B4, space between cells
5	Andrew	Brown	Andrew Brown	=PROPER(A5&" "&B5)	Initial caps, join cells A5 & B5, space between cells
6	Bobby	Ainge	11	=LEN(A6&" "&B6)	Number of characters in cells A6 & B6 plus any hidden
7	bobby	ainge	Bobby Ainge	=TRIM(PROPER(A7&" "&B7)	No hidden characters, initial caps, display A7 & B7

Figure 179

Functions are organised by category, such as Text and Logical (whether an argument is true or false), an argument can be numbers, text, logical values, tables or functions. A function is made up of **Function_Name(argument1, argument2 .....)**, an argument is the information that a function uses to produce a **New Value** or perform an action.

Function Wizard

The Function Wizard provides an easy guide to creating all formulas.

1. Click in a cell, choose Formulas , Insert Function

2. The Insert Function dialog box appears

3. In the **S**earch for a function box type "Text in Upper Case", press Go

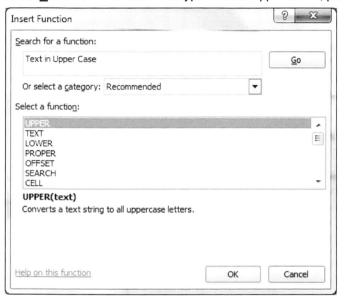

Figure 180

4. Click OK , the Function Arguments dialog box appears

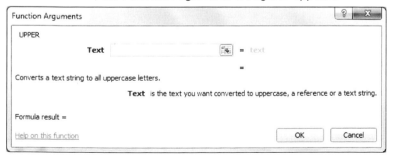

Figure 181

5. In the Text box type smart pc guides, click OK

6. The text appears in uppercase, the formula is =UPPER("smart pc guides")

Exercise 9: - Using the Function Wizard

1. Create the following table in a new worksheet

2. Using the Function Wizard and Quick Reference Formula

Department	Names	Quick Reference
Human Resources		Create in Uppercase
CreDit CONtroller	ANNe SparRow	Create in Proper Case
PRoject OfFiceR	JUDY Crow	Create in Proper Case
HR Clerk	HaRry Swift	Create in Uppercase
FinaNCe oFficer	JOHN starling	Create in Lowercase

3. Insert a column to display a copy of each working formula

4. The results from the exercise are displayed below

Department	Names
HUMAN RESOURCES	
Credit Controller	Anne Sparrow
Project Officer	Judy Crow
HR CLERK	HARRY SWIFT
finance officer	john starling

5. Save the worksheet Working with the Function Wizard

Search and Find Functions

The search function defined as *Search* is not case sensitive and allows a character or text string to be located, whereas the find function *Find* can locate a character or text string but is case sensitive.

Working with Search and Find

The following table provides a brief example of how the search and find functions work. It is important to plan the formula; brackets are colour coded =((( ))) when opened brackets are applied equal amounts of closed brackets need be used.

	A	B	C	D
2	SMART GUIDES	6	=SEARCH(" ",A2)	Search & display number of characters to space in cell
3	SMART GUIDES	6	=FIND(" ",A3)	Find & display number of characters to space in cell
4	SMART GUIDES	12	=LEN(A4)	Display number of characters in cell A4
5	SMART GUIDES	6	=LEN(A5)-SEARCH(" ",A5)	Search & display number of characters after the space
6	SMART GUIDES	6	=LEN(A6)-FIND(" ",A6)	Find & display number of characters after the space
7	SMART GUIDES	GUIDES	=RIGHT(A7,LEN(A7)-SEARCH(" ",A7))	Search & display from the right number of characters
8	SMART GUIDES	GUIDES	=RIGHT(A8,LEN(A8)-FIND(" ",A8))	Find & display from the right characters after the space
9	SMART GUIDES	SMART	=LEFT(A9,SEARCH(" ",A9))	Search & display characters to the left of the space
10	SMART GUIDES	SMART	=LEFT(A10,FIND(" ",A10))	Find & display characters to the left of the space
11	SMART GUIDES	Smart	=PROPER(LEFT(A11,SEARCH(" ",A11)))	Characters to the left of the space in initial caps
12	SMART GUIDES	Guides	=PROPER(RIGHT(A12,LEN(A12)-FIND(" ",A12)))	Characters after the space in intital caps

Figure 182

Exercise 10: - Working with Search and Find

1. Open a new workbook
2. Type out your first name and surname in a cell of your choice
3. Showing working formulas, find the number of characters in the cell
4. Find the number of characters from the left of the space
5. Search and display in lowercase the characters to the right of the space
6. Search and display in uppercase the characters to the left of the space
7. Save the workbook as Search and Find

Logical Functions

The **IF** function allows users to construct and analyse a formula's validity performing an action that calculates whether a statement is TRUE or FALSE. Up to seven **IF** statements can be grouped together (Nested) to construct a more detailed result. To test a statement, Excel evaluates a logical equation returning the word TRUE if the formula statement is true or FALSE if the statement is false.

Description	Symbol Used
Equal to	=
Greater than	>
Less than	<
Not equal to	<>
Greater than or equal to	>=
Less than or equal to	<=

Figure 183

IF Function

1. Open a new workbook, create the following information

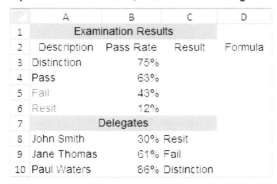

Figure 184

2. Select cell C8, following the formula below, generate the results for the 3 delegates

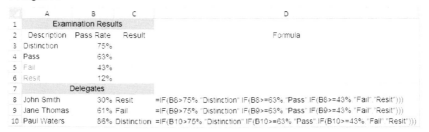

Figure 185

3. Save the workbook as Working with Nested Statements

Exercise 11: - Creating Nested Statements

1. Open a new workbook
2. Create a table displaying bank interest rates on a current account
3. Use the following rates

Rates	
2%	<=1000
3%	>2000
4%	>4345
5%	>6420

Note: **When using IF statements work from the HIGHEST VALUE downwards, make sure the percentage values are between inverted commas.**

4. Create IF Statements for the following amounts

Current Account (£)
2000
4500
6690
63

5. Save the workbook Working with Nested Statements

Outlining

Excel allows the user to create summary reports by using the Outline Function to show or hide data by grouping data by column or rows using Automatic Outline or Manual Outline.

Creating an Automatic Outline

1. Open a new workbook
2. Create the following information

	A	B	C	D	E	F	G	H	I	J
1		January	February	March	QTR 1 Total	April	May	June	QTR 2 Total	Grand Total
2	Sales Team A	£12 567	£13 987	£14 654	£41,208	£11 346	£12 432	£14 165	£37,943	£79,151
3	Sales Team B	£13 909	£12 976	£11 456	£38,341	£10 954	£11 675	£9 197	£31,826	£70,167
4	Sales Team C	£12 543	£12 788	£11 676	£37,007	£13 543	£10 456	£9 329	£33,328	£70,335
5	Sales Team D	£11 905	£12 765	£11 324	£35,994	£10 469	£11 232	£11 190	£32,891	£68,885
6	**Total Sales**	**£50,924**	**£52,516**	**£49,110**	**£152,550**	**£46,312**	**£45,795**	**£43,881**	**£135,988**	**£288,538**

Figure 186

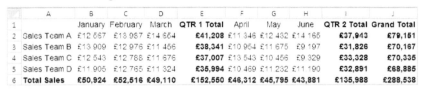

3. Click in the data to be outlined, Choose, Data , Group ▾ , Auto Outline

	A	B	C	D	E	F	G	H	I	J
1		January	February	March	QTR 1 Total	April	May	June	QTR 2 Total	Grand Total
2	Sales Team A	£12 567	£13 987	£14 654	£41,208	£11 346	£12 432	£14 165	£37,943	£79,151
3	Sales Team B	£13 909	£12 976	£11 456	£38,341	£10 954	£11 675	£9 197	£31,826	£70,167
4	Sales Team C	£12 543	£12 788	£11 676	£37,007	£13 543	£10 456	£9 329	£33,328	£70,335
5	Sales Team D	£11 905	£12 765	£11 324	£35,994	£10 469	£11 232	£11 190	£32,891	£68,885
6	**Total Sales**	**£50,924**	**£52,516**	**£49,110**	**£152,550**	**£46,312**	**£45,795**	**£43,881**	**£135,988**	**£288,538**

Figure 187

4. The horizontal outlines are displayed above the column

5. The vertical outlines are displayed to the left of the rows

6. In the horizontal area, choose 1 to view Grand Totals

7. The + sign indicates that there is more information that can be displayed

8. Click on the + to expand hidden information

9. The − indicates that all information is displayed

10. Click − to collapse and hide grouped information

11. Press 2 this displays Qtr 1, Qtr 2 and Grand Totals

12. Choose 3 to display all the information

13. Repeat the process for the Vertical Outline area

14. To clear the outline select Data , Ungroup ▾ , Clear Outline

15. Save the workbook as Using Outlines

Exercise 12: - Creating a Manual Outline

Manual Outline allows the user to control information that is to be grouped together. It can also be used in conjunction with the Automatic Outline.

1. Open the workbook Using Outlines

2. Select cells B1:D1

3. Choose Data , Group , → Group...

4. The Group dialog box appears

5. Select Columns

6. Click OK

7. Repeat the process for cell F1:H1

8. The horizontal outlines are displayed above the columns headings

9. Select B1:I1, create a Manual Column Outline

10. Select A2:A5, group the rows to create a Vertical Outline

11. Save the workbook Using Outlines

Data Consolidation

Using the Consolidation Feature allows data to be combined using independent workbooks or different worksheets.

1. Open a new workbook

2. In the worksheet create the following using formulas where applicable

	A	B	C	D	E	F
1			MS Office 2002			
2		Qtr 1	Qtr 2	Qtr 3	Qtr 4	Total
3	Word	100	200	300	400	1000
4	Excel	100	200	300	40	640
5	PowerPoint	75	75	80	125	355
6	Access	50	40	35	27	152
7	Project	25	40	50	60	175

Figure 188

3. Highlight cells A2:F7, select Formulas , Define Name ▾

4. Alternatively [Alt] [M] [M] [D] displays the New Name dialog box

5. Type the name as Table, press [OK]

6. Create a New folder named Consolidation to store the workbooks

7. Save the workbook as MS Office 2002, close the workbook

8. Repeat the process for MS Office 2003 and MS Office 2007

	A	B	C	D	E	F
1			MS Office 2003			
2		Qtr 1	Qtr 2	Qtr 3	Qtr 4	Total
3	Word	100	200	300	400	1000
4	Excel	100	200	300	40	640
5	PowerPoint	75	75	80	125	355
6	Access	50	40	35	27	152
7	Project	25	40	50	60	175

Figure 189

	A	B	C	D	E	F
1			MS Office 2007			
2		Qtr 1	Qtr 2	Qtr 3	Qtr 4	Total
3	Word	100	200	300	400	1000
4	Excel	100	200	300	40	640
5	PowerPoint	75	75	80	125	355
6	Access	50	40	35	27	152
7	Project	25	40	50	60	175

Figure 190

9. Ensure the workbooks MS Office 2002, 2003 and 2007 are open

10. Open a new workbook, select cell A1

11. Select Data , Consolidate , the Consolidate dialog box appears

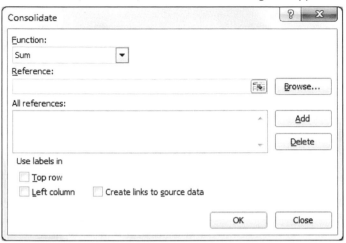

Figure 191

12. In the Function area select SUM

13. Press Browse... to locate MS Office 2002

14. Select the file, choose OK

Figure 192

15. Click on the Reference icon

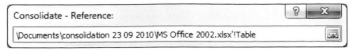

Figure 193

16. After the exclamation mark type Table

17. Select the icon [icon] to return to the Consolidate dialog box

18. Click [Add] to save the reference

19. Repeat steps 13 to 18 for MS Office 2003 and MS Office 2007

20. Select Use labels in, tick Top row and Left column

21. Tick Create links to source data as shown

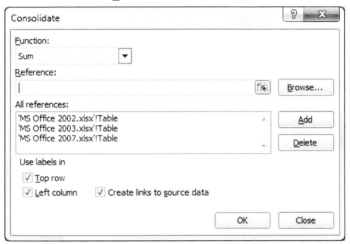

Figure 194

22. Select [OK], the consolidated worksheet appears

1 2		A	C	D	E	F	G
	1		Qtr 1	Qtr 2	Qtr 3	Qtr 4	Total
+	5	Word	300	600	900	1200	3000
+	9	Excel	300	600	900	120	1920
+	13	PowerPoint	225	225	240	375	1065
+	17	Access	150	120	105	81	456
+	21	Project	75	120	150	180	525

Figure 195

23. Use the outline ⊞ and ⊟ signs to reveal or collapse the linked data

24. Save the workbook as Consolidation of Data

25. Close all the workbooks

26. Re-open the Consolidation of Data workbook

27. The following security warning appears

> ⚠ **Security Warning**   Automatic update of links has been disabled | Enable Content |

Figure 196

28. Select | Enable Content |

29. When the consolidated worksheet is re-opened, the following prompt appears

Figure 197

30. Choose | Update | to view the workbook

31. Close the workbook

Templates

A template is a means of creating a workbook that is consistent allowing such documents as Invoices, Timesheets and Balance Sheets to be used with pre-set styles and formatting. When a new workbook is generated as a template it is used as the basis for the worksheet. Templates are saved to the Normal general area; however, it is possible to create a new tab for an organisation in the templates area that allows company templates to be quickly identified.

Save a Workbook as a Template

1. Select | File |, choose | Save As |

2. Save as Smart PC Guides Timesheet

3. Click on the downward pointing arrow ▼ i   n the Save as type: area

4. Select Excel Template to move to the Templates area

Figure 198

5. In the Template folder, click on the New folder icon

6. In the <u>N</u>ame area type Smart PC Guides Template

7. Press Enter

8. Save and close the template

9. To view the template select File , New

My templates

10. Select   Choose the Tab Smart PC Guides Templates

Figure 199

11. Select the Smart PC Guides Timesheet Template

12. Click OK to open a new workbook based on the template

Exercise 13: - Open and Amend an Existing Template

This exercise demonstrates how to customise a template quickly.

1. Choose 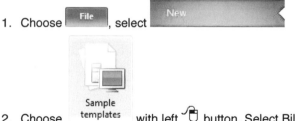 File , select New

2. Choose Sample templates with left 🖱 button, Select Billing Statement

3. Change the font to Arial 10 with a Blue Bold font colour

4. In cell B1 replace Your Company Name with Smart PC Guides

5. In cell B4 change Zip Code to Post Code

6. In cell F12 change Zip Code to Post Code

7. In cells H15 and H16 change the currency to £ symbol

8. In cell C25 change the currency to £ symbol

9. Select Review

10. Choose Protect Sheet , click OK

11. Name the template as Smart PC Guides Billing Statement

12. Save the template in the Smart PC Guides Template area

13. Close the workbook

14. Re-open the template from the Smart PC Guides Templates Tab

Scenario Manager

The Scenario Manager is part of the What If analysis. Each scenario added to the Scenario Manager has a defined name applied to the data. By grouping data, it is possible to use the Scenario Manager to display the outcome of what will happen to the worksheet if the data from a scenario is applied.

Creating Scenarios in a Workbook

1. Open a new workbook

2. Create the following information, insert the formulas in cells B9 and B11

3. Name the worksheet Project Expenses

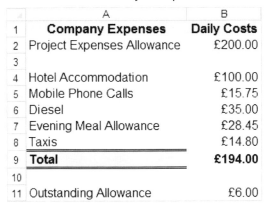

	A	B
1	**Company Expenses**	**Daily Costs**
2	Project Expenses Allowance	£200.00
3		
4	Hotel Accommodation	£100.00
5	Mobile Phone Calls	£15.75
6	Diesel	£35.00
7	Evening Meal Allowance	£28.45
8	Taxis	£14.80
9	**Total**	**£194.00**
10		
11	Outstanding Allowance	£6.00

Figure 200

4. Select cell B2, choose Formulas , Define Name ▾

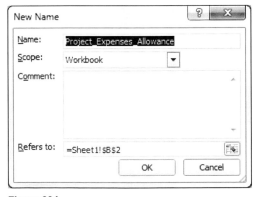

Figure 201

5. Click OK

6. Repeat steps 4 and 5 for cells B4:B9 and B11

7. Select Name Manager, the Name Manager dialog box appear

8. Alternatively ⎡CTRL⎤ ⎡F3⎤ displays the Name Manager dialog box

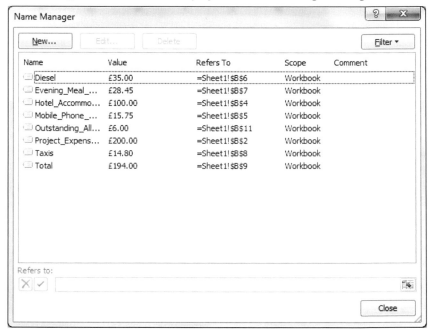

Figure 202

9. Click [Close]

10. Select [Data], click the left 🖱 button on the arrow in What-If Analysis ▾

11. Press the option Scenario Manager

Figure 203

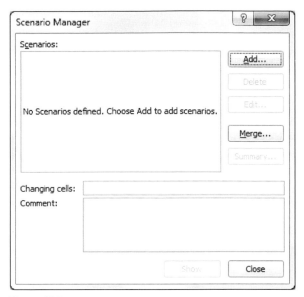

Figure 204

12. Press

13. Type Normal Values in the Scenario <u>n</u>ame area

14. Select the icon, highlight cells B2, B4:B8

15. Press to return to the Edit Scenario dialog box

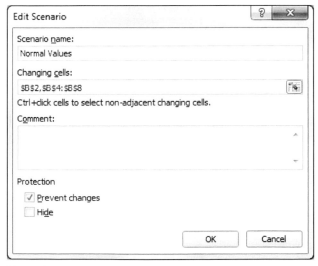

Figure 205

16. Click 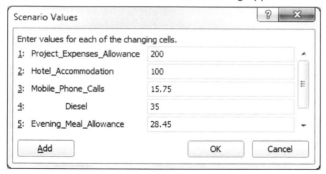 the Scenario Values dialog appears

Figure 206

17. Click  to return to the Scenario Manager dialog box

Figure 207

18. Repeat steps 12 to 17 to generate a Most Expensive Scenario

19. Update the values as shown on the next page

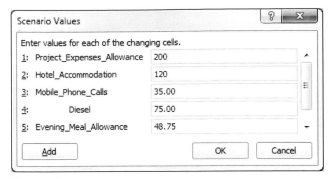

Figure 208

20. Click OK to display the Scenario Manager dialog box

21. Create a Least Expensive Scenario, update the values as shown below

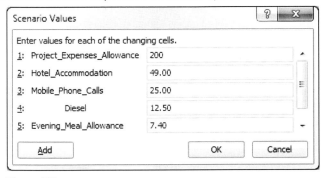

Figure 209

22. Click OK to display the Scenario Manager dialog box

Displaying Scenarios

1. Choose the Most Expensive Scenario, click [Show]

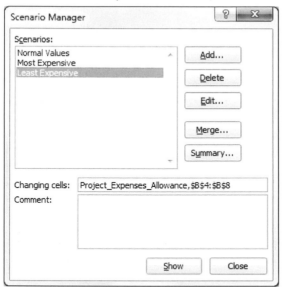

Figure 210

2. The data in the worksheet changes and is displayed

	A	B
1	**Company Expenses**	**Daily Costs**
2	Project Expenses Allowance	£200.00
3		
4	Hotel Accommodation	£120.00
5	Mobile Phone Calls	£35.00
6	Diesel	£75.00
7	Evening Meal Allowance	£48.75
8	Taxis	£14.80
9	**Total**	**£293.55**
10		
11	Outstanding Allowance	-£93.55

Figure 211

3. Repeat the process for the other scenarios

4. Re-select the Scenario Normal Values, press [Show]

5. To view a summary of the results select [Summary...]

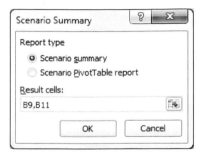

Figure 212

6. Choose Report type Scenario **s**ummary

7. In the **R**esults cells area ensure cell B9 and B11 are selected

8. Click [OK]

9. The Scenario Summary is displayed on a separate worksheet

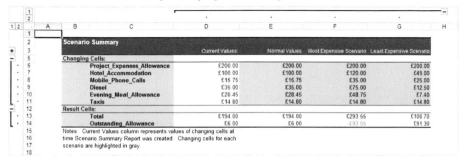

Figure 213

10. Vertical and Horizontal Outlines enable data to be expanded or collapsed

11. Save the Workbook as Creating Scenarios, close the workbook

Custom Views

Custom Views enables the user to store, format and print options by selection and applies a name to a particular view.

Creating a Custom View

1. Open the workbook Creating Scenarios
2. Select the worksheet named Project Expenses
3. Highlight cells A1:B11

4. Select   View ,   Custom Views

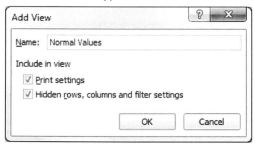

Figure 214

5. Click   Add... , type the name as Normal Values, click   OK

Figure 215

6. Choose the worksheet named Scenario Summary, highlight cells B2:G13

7. Select   View ,   Custom Views , the Custom Views dialog box appears
8. Press   Add... , name as Scenario Summary Sheet, click   OK
9. Save to update the workbook Creating Scenarios

`Displaying a Custom View

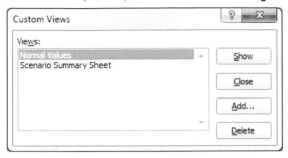

1. Select View , Custom Views , the Custom Views dialog box appears

Figure 216

2. Select the view to be displayed

3. Click [Show], the defined area is displayed and highlighted

PivotTables

The PivotTable Function allows data to be viewed from a different perspective. The report appears in a table format whereby the user decides the location of the data within the workbook.   The PivotTable Function automatically applies formatting to the information used. All PivotTables need to be planned to decide what information needs to be displayed.

Creating a PivotTable

1. Open up a new workbook, create the following information

	A	B	C	D	E	F
1	**Name**	**Staff ID**	**Date Hired**	**Department**	**Job Title**	**Current Salary**
2	Paul Smith	1	10/01/1965	Marketing	Marketing Administrator	£15,122.00
3	Jane Barrow	2	11/02/1999	Sales	Sector Director	£43,300.00
4	Rachael Jones	3	04/03/1990	IT	IT Helpdesk	£23,578.00
5	Robert Williams	4	03/02/2000	Human Resources	HR Manager	£30,500.00
6	James Harrow	5	22/04/1996	Marketing	Brand Manager	£27,498.00
7	Hannah Brown	6	10/07/1997	Marketing	Marketing Assistant	£12,750.00
8	Ruth Powers	7	21/02/1976	Accounts	Account Handler	£16,029.00

Figure 217

2. Click in the data area

3. Select Insert , PivotTable , PivotTable

4. A moving dotted line appears around the selected data

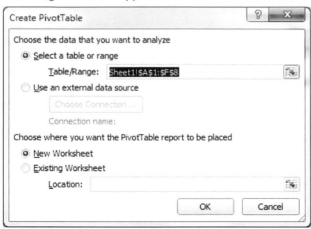

Figure 218

5. Ensure ⊙ New Worksheet is selected

6. Click   OK

Figure 219

7. The PivotTable Field list appears on the right hand side of the worksheet

8. From the PivotTable Field list select Name with the left 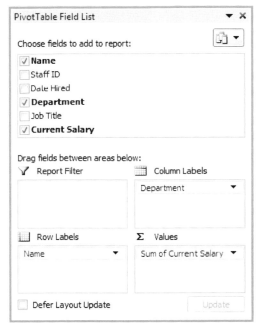 button

9. Drag the mouse pointer ⇧ to the Row Labels field box, release the mouse

10. Repeat the process moving Department to Column Labels

11. Current Salary to Values

Figure 220

12. Data is automatically placed in the PivotTable on the left of the worksheet

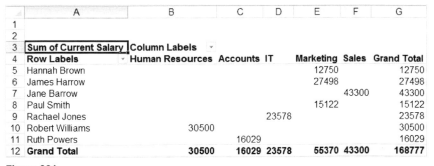

	A	B	C	D	E	F	G
1							
2							
3	Sum of Current Salary	Column Labels					
4	Row Labels	Human Resources	Accounts	IT	Marketing	Sales	Grand Total
5	Hannah Brown				12750		12750
6	James Harrow				27498		27498
7	Jane Barrow					43300	43300
8	Paul Smith				15122		15122
9	Rachael Jones			23578			23578
10	Robert Williams	30500					30500
11	Ruth Powers		16029				16029
12	**Grand Total**	**30500**	**16029**	**23578**	**55370**	**43300**	**168777**

Figure 221

13. From the PivotTable Field list click the left button on Sum of Current Salary ▼

14. Select 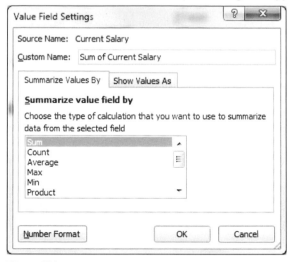 Value Field Settings... , the dialog box appears

Value Field Settings

Source Name: Current Salary

Custom Name: Sum of Current Salary

Summarize Values By | Show Values As

Summarize value field by

Choose the type of calculation that you want to use to summarize
data from the selected field

Sum
Count
Average
Max
Min
Product

Number Format   OK   Cancel

Figure 222

15. Select Number Format , choose currency decimal places two

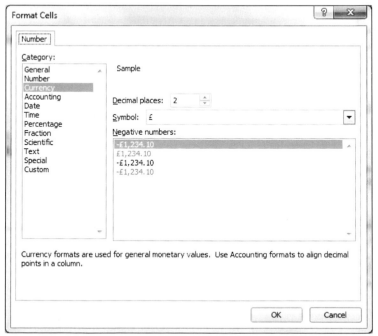

Format Cells

Number

Category:

General
Number
Currency
Accounting
Date
Time
Percentage
Fraction
Scientific
Text
Special
Custom

Sample

Decimal places: 2

Symbol: £

Negative numbers:

-£1,234.10
£1,234.10
-£1,234.10
-£1,234.10

Currency formats are used for general monetary values. Use Accounting formats to align decimal
points in a column.

OK   Cancel

Figure 223

16. Press [OK] twice

17. The PivotTable displays the currency format

18. Save the workbook as Working with PivotTables

Changing Data in a PivotTable

1. Click on the downward arrow on the |Column Labels ▼| in the PivotTable

2. The menu expands, click with the left 🖱 button on ☑ (Select All)

3. The criteria is deselected

4. Click with the left 🖱 button to place a tick for ☑ Marketing

5. Press [OK]

6. The PivotTable displays the staff in Marketing

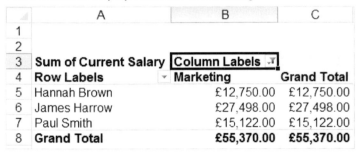

	A	B	C
1			
2			
3	**Sum of Current Salary**	**Column Labels** ▼	
4	**Row Labels** ▼	**Marketing**	**Grand Total**
5	Hannah Brown	£12,750.00	£12,750.00
6	James Harrow	£27,498.00	£27,498.00
7	Paul Smith	£15,122.00	£15,122.00
8	**Grand Total**	**£55,370.00**	**£55,370.00**

Figure 224

7. Repeat these steps to display the other departments

8. Information can be quickly restructured to display a different set of data

9. To display the data in a different format, for example staff in Marketing

10. From the PivotTable Field list click the left 🖱 button on Sum of Current Salary ▼

11. Select 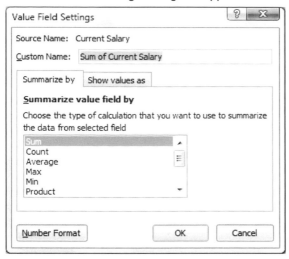 Value Field Settings...

12. The Value Field Settings dialog box appears

Figure 225

13. Choose Count, select the Number Format , select General

14. Press OK twice

15. The updated PivotTable displays the number of staff in Marketing

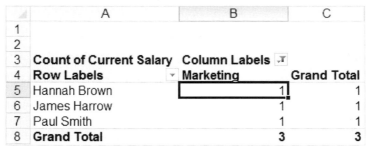

	A	B	C
1			
2			
3	**Count of Current Salary**	**Column Labels**	
4	**Row Labels**	**Marketing**	**Grand Total**
5	Hannah Brown	1	1
6	James Harrow	1	1
7	Paul Smith	1	1
8	**Grand Total**	**3**	**3**

Figure 226

16. Click on the downward arrow on the **Column Labels** in the PivotTable

17. Select Human Resources and IT, press OK

18. The PivotTable is updated displaying the members of staff from Marketing, Human Resources and IT

19. From the PivotTable Field list click the left 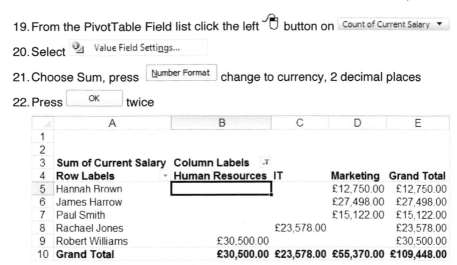 button on Count of Current Salary ▼

20. Select ⚙ Value Field Settings...

21. Choose Sum, press Number Format change to currency, 2 decimal places

22. Press OK twice

	A	B	C	D	E
1					
2					
3	Sum of Current Salary	Column Labels ⊤			
4	Row Labels ▾	Human Resources	IT	Marketing	Grand Total
5	Hannah Brown			£12,750.00	£12,750.00
6	James Harrow			£27,498.00	£27,498.00
7	Paul Smith			£15,122.00	£15,122.00
8	Rachael Jones		£23,578.00		£23,578.00
9	Robert Williams	£30,500.00			£30,500.00
10	Grand Total	£30,500.00	£23,578.00	£55,370.00	£109,448.00

Figure 227

Naming a PivotTable

1. Ensure the Options Tab is displayed from PivotTable Tools

2. Under PivotTable Name from the PivotTable Grouping, highlight PivotTable1 and replace the text with Smart PC Guides

Figure 228

3. Press Return or Enter, save the PivotTable

Refreshing Data in a PivotTable

1. Click in the original data created in Sheet1

2. Increase Paul Smith's salary to £17,250

3. Click back in the PivotTable

4. Select Options, choose Refresh or alternatively press ALT F5

5. The PivotTable is updated

6. Go back to the original data in Sheet1

7. Change Paul Smith's salary back to £15,122 and press Refresh

Show/Hide Field Headers

1. Click in the PivotTable data

2. Choose Options, select Field Headers from the Show Grouping, the Field Headers disappear

3. Click with the left button a second time to display the Field Headers

Show/Hide Field List

1. Click in the PivotTable data

2. Choose Options, select, Field List the Field List disappears

3. Click with the left button a second time to display the Field List

Creating a PivotChart from a PivotTable

1. Select Options from the  PivotTable Tools

2. Choose PivotChart from the Tools Grouping

3. The Insert Chart dialog box appears

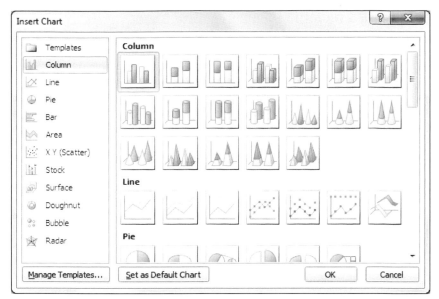

Figure 229

4. Select Clustered Cylinder, press [OK]

5. The Chart appears in the worksheet

Adding Additional Data to a PivotChart

1. Click on the downward arrow on the **Column Labels** ▾ in the PivotTable

2. Select ☑ Accounts , press [OK]

3. Data referring to Accounts appears in the PivotTable and PivotChart

4. Remove the accounts data from the PivotTable using **Column Labels** ▾

5. Save to update the workbook

Displaying a PivotChart on a Separate Sheet

1. Click anywhere in the PivotTable data

2. Press F11 , the chart appears in a separate worksheet named Chart1

3. Rename the worksheet named Chart1 to Smart PC Guides

4. Save the workbook

Customising a PivotChart

1. Click anywhere in the PivotTable data, highlight the staff in Marketing

2. Select Options , choose Group Selection

⇒ Group Selection

↳ Ungroup

📷 Group Field

 Group

Figure 230

3. Select the cell named Group1 the staff in Marketing

4. Rename Group1 with the name Marketing, press Return or Enter

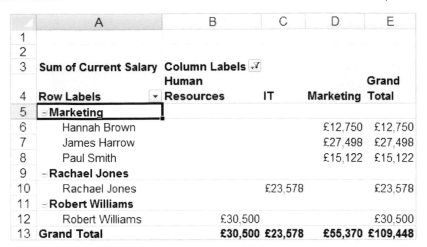

Sum of Current Salary	Column Labels ☑			
Row Labels ▾	Human Resources	IT	Marketing	Grand Total
– Marketing				
Hannah Brown			£12,750	£12,750
James Harrow			£27,498	£27,498
Paul Smith			£15,122	£15,122
– Rachael Jones				
Rachael Jones		£23,578		£23,578
– Robert Williams				
Robert Williams	£30,500			£30,500
Grand Total	£30,500	£23,578	£55,370	£109,448

Figure 231

5. Replace **– Rachael Jones** with IT, press Return or [Enter]

6. Replace **– Robert Williams** with Human Resources, press Return or [Enter]

7. Select the Sheet Tab named Smart PC Guides containing the PivotChart

8. Click anywhere in the chart, choose [Design] from the [PivotTable Tools]

9. From the Chart Layout Grouping select Layout 5

10. Change the Chart Title to Smart PC Guides

11. Change the Axis Title to Salary

12. Save the Workbook

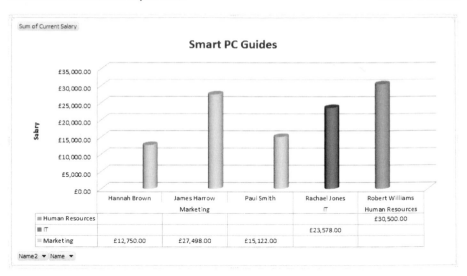

Sum of Current Salary

Smart PC Guides

	Hannah Brown	James Harrow	Paul Smith	Rachael Jones	Robert Williams
		Marketing		IT	Human Resources
■ Human Resources					£30,500.00
■ IT				£23,578.00	
■ Marketing	£12,750.00	£27,498.00	£15,122.00		

Name2 ▼ Name ▼

Figure 232

PivotTable Slicers

A Slicer can be used to quickly filter data in a PivotTable. The slicer includes a header, filtering buttons, a clear filter button, scroll bar, move and resize controls. A number of slicers can be used that can be moved around the worksheet. The slicers can also be formatted with styles to correspond with the look of the worksheet being used and can be used with multiple PivotTables.

1. Click in the data in the PivotTable

2. Select Options from the PivotTable Tools, choose Insert Slicer ▾

3. Select Insert Slicer... , the Insert Slicers dialog box appears

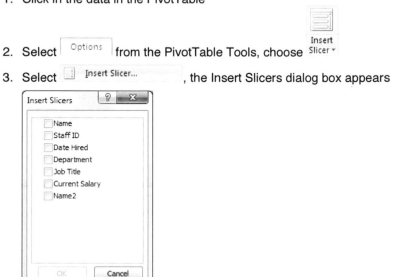

Figure 233

4. Click with the left  button, select Department

5. Press [OK], the Insert Slicer dialog box appears

Department ✖

Human Resources

Accounts

IT

Marketing

Sales

Figure 234

6. The highlighted fields are those currently represented in the PivotTable

7. If the slicer does not display all the data a vertical scroll bar appears

8. To resize or move the slicer click and drag on the borders

9. To remove the current filter select the Clear Filter icon ✖

10. Or press [ALT] [C]

11. The PivotTable displays all the data

12. Select [Human Resources] In the slicer with the left button

13. Hold the [CTRL] key down, select [IT] and [Marketing], release the [CTRL] key

14. The PivotTable and slicer displays the selected data

Format the Slicer

1. Click on the slicer

2. Choose [Options] from the Slicer Tools Tab

3. Select Slicer Styles, click on the downward point arrow ⬇ to expand the menu

Figure 235

4. Select the required style

Delete a Slicer

1. Click with the left 🖱 button to select the slicer

2. Press [Delete]

Macros

A Macro is a method of recording commands, keystrokes and actions that allow automated tasks. The macro recorder does not record in real time so the user can take the time to correctly complete each action.

Preparation Work before Recording a Macro

1. Write down each step of the macro
2. What should the macro do?
3. Where should the macro be stored?
4. Does the macro need to be available to other workbooks?
5. Does formatting need to be applied?
6. Does the macro need to be applied to specific cells (absolute)?
7. Does the macro need to be applied to any cells (relative)?
8. Provide an appropriate name to identify the macro
9. Do a walkthrough of the steps before recording the macro

Creating a Relative Reference Macro to Format Cells

1. Select

2. The Record Macro dialog box appears

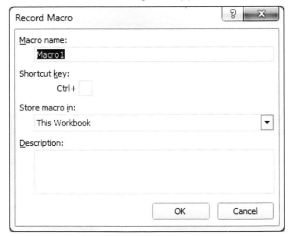

Figure 236

3. Name the macro as Formatting_Cells

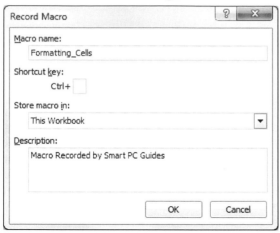

Figure 237

4. Store the macro in This Workbook (the macro is available only in this workbook)

5. Use the description area to describe the Macro being created

6. Choose | OK |

7. ☐ | A macro is currently recording. Click to stop recording. | appears in the Status Bar area

8. To apply relative referencing click on | View |

9. Choose

10. The border of the icon changes to orange [icon] when Use Relative References is applied

11. Click in cell A1

12. Press | CTRL | | 1 | to display the Format Cells dialog

13. Select the Font Tab, change the Colour to Blue

14. Select the Number Tab, set the options as shown

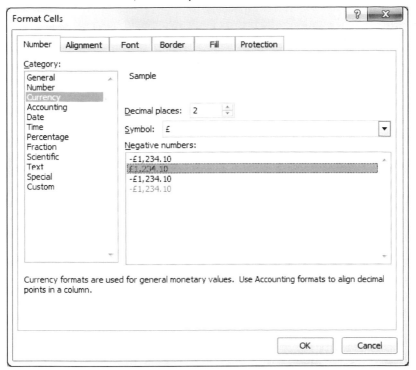

Figure 238

15. Click [OK]

16. Press

17. In cell A1, type 45, press Return or [Enter]

18. 45 has changed to £45.00 in blue font

19. Delete the information in A1, type -6, press Return, [£6.00] appears in red

20. In a series of cells type the following numbers

	A	B	C	D	E	F
4	Sales A	1	2	3	4	5
5	Sales B	6	7	8	9	10
6						
7	Total	7	9	11	13	15

Figure 239

21. Select the cells containing the numbers

22. Press ALT F8 to display the Macro dialog box

Figure 240

23. Choose the macro named Formatting_Cells

24. Select Run , the numbers are formatted automatically using the macro

Deleting a Macro

1. Select ALT F8

2. Choose the macro to be deleted, select Delete

3. The following dialog box appears

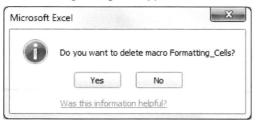

Figure 241

4. Choose Yes , the macro is deleted

Note: If the Macro has been saved in the PERSONAL.XLSB area you will need to unhide the workbook using the unhide command found under the View command.

Exercise 14: - Creating a Header and Footer Macro

1. Create a macro and name it Header_Footer

2. Store the macro in Personal Macro Workbook (the macro is available whenever Excel is used)

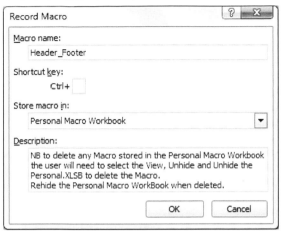

3. Type and centre a heading named **Smart PC Guides**

4. In the bottom left Footer area type **V1.0**

5. In the Centre Footer area type Page &[Page] of &[Pages]

6. In the bottom right Footer area choose Current Date press spacebar and Current Time

7. Click Stop Recording

8. Click on a new workbook

9. In cell A1 type =Today() to insert the date

10. Select View, Macros, View Macros

11. Run the macro named Header_Footer

12. Preview the results

Creating a Relative Reference Macro for a Web Address

To create a macro to produce a company Web address, widen the column to display the address in the cell and the macro stored in the Personal.xls Macro Workbook. When the Macro is stored in the Personal macro workbook, it can used with any workbook.

1. Select  , Record Macro...

2. The Record Macro dialog box appears

Figure 242

3. Name the macro as WebAddress

4. Store the macro in This Workbook

5. Choose [OK]

6. [▪] [A macro is currently recording. Click to stop recording.] appears in the Status Bar area

7. Select View , Macros ▾

8. Ensure an orange border is around [⊞] Use Relative References to show it is activated

9. Select cell A1, press

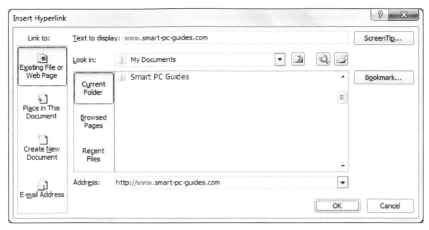

Figure 243

10. Complete the **T**ext to display and Add**r**ess boxes, press OK

11. Widen the column to fit the web address in the cell

12. Select View , Macros , Stop **R**ecording

13. Press View , Macros , **V**iew Macros or press ALT F8

14. Select All Open Workbooks

Figure 244

15. Select **Personal.XLSB!Web_Address**

16. Press  Run ⎵ to view the results of the macro

Quick Access Toolbar

The Quick Access Toolbar keeps commands that are frequently used. The items are readily available regardless of which of the Ribbon's Tabs a user is working in. The Quick Access Toolbar is located above the ribbon (default)

or below The Ribbon

Figure 245   **Figure 246**

Displaying the Quick Access Toolbar below the Ribbon

1. Click with the left 🖰 button on the downward pointing arrow ▾ to open the Customise Quick Access Toolbar menu

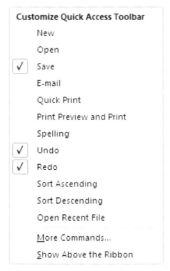

Figure 247

2. Click with the left 🖰 button on ✓ Print Preview and Print

3. The Print Preview and Print Icon 🔍 is displayed on the toolbar

4. Press ⎵ ESC ⎵ to return to the workbook

5. Click with the left 🖰 button on the downward pointing arrow ▾

6. Select   More Commands...

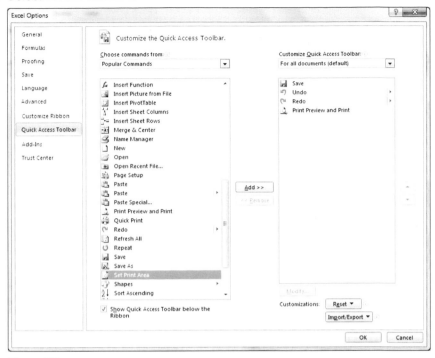

Figure 248

7. From the Popular Commands select Set Print Area, press [Add >>]

8. The feature is now displayed in the Quick Access Toolbar area

9. Reposition items using the [▲] and [▼] arrows

10. Click Popular Commands [▼], the menu is expanded

11. Click [OK]

Removing a Command from the Quick Access Toolbar

1. Press with the right 🖰 button over the command to be removed

2. Click   Remove from Quick Access Toolbar

3. The command is removed from the Quick Access Toolbar

Excel File Formats

Excel 2010 uses file formats that are different from those used in previous versions of Excel. By not using the new formats some of the new features of Excel 2010 may be lost.

Formats used in Excel 2010

Excel Workbook: The new binary workbook format that enables the new features of Excel 2010 and that also speeds up your work. Files saved in this format cannot be opened in earlier versions of Excel unless the translating filter programme has been downloaded. The new binary workbook format will be seen with an added x, for example **.xlsx**

Excel Macro-Enabled Workbook: This format is the same as the Workbook format with the addition of macros. This format will be saved as **.xlsm**

Excel Template: A new form of template in Excel 2010 that enables the new features of the programme. The new format will be saved with an added x, for example **.xltx**

Excel Macro-Enables Template: This format is the same as the Excel Template with the addition of macros. The new format will be saved with an added x, for example **.xltxm**

Excel 97-2003 Format: The binary format used in previous versions of Excel. Using this format disables some of the new features of Excel 2010. This format will be saved as **.xls**

Excel 97-2003 Format Template: The binary file format for templates used in previous versions of Excel. This format will be saved as **.xlt**

Single File Web Page: This format is used to create a web page and stores the graphics in the same file.

Web Page: Creates a standard HTML-format web page where graphics are stored on a separate file. This format will be saved as **.htm**

This concludes the Excel 2010 Foundation to Expert Guide. Thank you for choosing Smart PC Guides. Please visit our website www.smart-pc-guides.com to view our complete range of Smart PC Guides.

Shortcut Keys

SHORTCUT KEYS		DESCRIPTION	SHORTCUT KEYS		DESCRIPTION
CTRL	F1	Hide/Display the Ribbon	F1		Excel Help
CTRL	F2	Displays Print Preview	F2		Edit Active Cell
CTRL	—	Delete Cells, Rows, Columns	F5		Go To Dialog Box
CTRL	1	Format Cells	F7		Spell Checker
CTRL	2	Apply/Remove Bold Format	F10		Displays Shortcut Keys
CTRL	3	Apply/Remove Italic Format	F11		Creates a Chart
CTRL	4	Apply/Remove Underline	F12		Save As Dialog Box
CTRL	5	Apply/Remove Strikethrough	ALT M D		Trace Dependents
CTRL	B	Apply/Remove Bold Format	ALT M P		Trace Precedents
CTRL	C	Copy Cells	ALT M W		Watch Window Dialog Box
CTRL	P	Displays Print Dialog Box	ALT W P		Page Layout View
CTRL	S	Saves the Workbook	ALT	F8	Macro Dialog Box
CTRL	U	Apply/Remove Underline	CTRL	F3	Displays Name Manager
CTRL	V	Paste Cells	CTRL SHIFT $		Currency 2 Decimal Places
CTRL	X	Cuts Information	CTRL SHIFT !		Number 2 Decimal Places
CTRL	Y	Repeats Previous Command	CTRL SHIFT +		Insert Cells, Rows, Columns
CTRL	Z	Undo Previous Command	CTRL SHIFT P		Format Cells Dialog Box
SHIFT	F2	Insert Comment Dialog Box	SHIFT	F3	Insert Function Dialog Box

Index